A COMMENTARY ON
WORDSWORTH'S
PRELUDE
BOOKS I-V

A COMMENTARY ON
WORDSWORTH'S
PRELUDE
BOOKS I-V

TED HOLT
JOHN GILROY

Routledge & Kegan Paul
London, Boston, Melbourne and Henley

First published in 1983
by Routledge & Kegan Paul plc
39 Store Street, London WC1E 7DD
9 Park Street, Boston, Mass. 02108, USA,
464 St Kilda Road, Melbourne,
Victoria 3004, Australia, and
Broadway House, Newtown Road,
Henley-on-Thames, Oxon RG9 1EN
Photoset in 11 on 13 Garamond by
Kelly Typesetting Ltd, Bradford-on-Avon, Wiltshire
and printed in Great Britain by
The Thetford Press Ltd, Thetford, Norfolk

Library of Congress Cataloging in Publication Data

Holt, Ted, 1943–
A commentary on Wordsworth's Prelude, Books I–V.

Includes bibliographical references
1. Wordsworth, William, 1770–1850. The Prelude
I. Gilroy, John, 1946– . II. Title.
PR5864.H64 1983   821'.7   83–10897

ISBN 0–7100–9569–4 (pbk)

To our parents, Mary, Jane, and the children

Contents

Preface   ix

Acknowledgments   xi

Book I   1

Book II   32

Book III   56

Book IV   79

Book V   99

Notes   123

Preface

This book provides a commentary on *The Prelude* of 1805, Books I–V. It follows Wordsworth's division of his poem into verse-paragraphs and their arrangement in the Norton Critical Edition (1979). The reader is asked to consider a whole verse-paragraph closely and then refer to the commentary. It is essential to use this book in direct association with the text of *The Prelude*, considering each paragraph in turn. We do not intend it to be a crib, imposing its own limitations upon the poem, but a continuous reading which may offer opportunities for further enjoyment.

As a reading, it seeks to present the poem as a continuous whole. Many readers know *The Prelude* only in extract or think of it merely as a succession of high points linked by much that has been called tedious or even irrelevant. We have pointed attention, therefore, not only to individual passages but to the developing argument into which they fit. Taking our cue from Wordsworth, we have attended to the 'parts/As parts' (VII: 712–13) but taken care to sustain 'a feeling of the whole' (VII: 713). It seems to us that the poem asks for such a double attentiveness. This approach implies some level of response to the subtle arranging of the verse-paragraphs so as to allow for a cumulative sense of argument. We have appended a brief concluding paragraph to each Book in order to summarise the pattern of its thought.

Awareness of the actual paragraph sequence may allow for a

much better understanding of particular passages usually studied in complete isolation, such as the boating and skating episodes in Book I, the encounter with the soldier in Book IV, or the Winander Boy passage in Book V. Such episodes are better understood individually if related to what precedes them; placing in the argument is vitally important. Awareness of sequence is particularly urgent when Wordsworth clearly sets one paragraph against another in a pattern of antithesis. Attention upon the isolated passage then misses much of the Poet's point. Antithetical patterning is very marked in the opening paragraphs of Book I (1–271) where it dramatises opposing attitudes to the composition of the poem and the crux of the argument in Book IV is presented in two paragraphs of entirely opposed viewpoint (247–304 and 304–45). Wordsworth sometimes uses classical dualities (thesis and antithesis) to present the experience of being in two minds about an issue. This is one of the ways in which the paragraphing makes a crucial contribution to the sense.

The Prelude does not, however, possess the linear quality of simple narrative verse and this is because it proceeds through its verse-paragraphs in quantum-jumps of poetic energy, rather than straightforwardly through the lines. For this reason, we have dealt with each paragraph as a coherent whole, with its own tone, language, viewpoint, and atmosphere. Above all, we intend this commentary as an aid to enjoyment of *The Prelude*. Though widely accepted as Wordsworth's masterpiece, it continues to enjoy the status of a poem respected rather than read, or, at best, read unevenly. We hope that this commentary will do something towards helping students find a way into, and through, this most original and exciting poem.

Acknowledgments

The authors would like to thank Sydney Bolt and John Wilkinson of CCAT, Cambridge for some perceptive and helpful comments, and Mrs Wraith for typing the manuscript. Our thanks are also due to Henry Merritt who 'surely met with strange adventures'.

Acknowledgments

BOOK I

Lines 1–32

The poem opens with a deep sigh of release. The peaceful liberating influence of the 'gentle breeze' (1) is introduced by Wordsworth's own expending breath. The breeze is synonymous with freedom and blows from 'the green fields and from the clouds/And from the sky' (2–3). There is an immediate opening out in terms of both height and breadth ('fields . . . clouds . . . sky'), which conveys the exhilaration of having no direction and being totally free. The Poet feels a sympathy with the breeze because it is as homeless and as liberated as himself. It is as though it answers his mood, 'seems half conscious of the joy it gives' (4), leading on to his excited recognition, 'O welcome messenger! O welcome friend!' (5). Set against this ecstatic mood of peace and gentleness is the harsh and punitive concept of the city as 'prison' (8) where he has been a 'captive' (6). Words which express restriction, 'bondage', 'walls' (7), 'immured' (8), are placed against notions of absolute freedom. He emerges, like the prisoners in *Fidelio*, from captivity – 'Now I am free, enfranchised and at large' (9). Enfranchised was a word used particularly in connection with freed slaves, and 'house/Of bondage' (6–7) reminds us specifically of the Israelites led by Moses out of slavery in Egypt ('I am the Lord thy God, which have brought thee out of the land of Egypt, out of the house of bondage.' Exodus 20:2). Potentially enclosing words in the rhetorical questions which follow, 'dwelling', 'vale' (11), 'harbour' (12), are lightly passed over, while the unanswered questions themselves create a sense of numerous possibilities left intact. The commitment involved by making a single choice is excluded.

Although he echoes *Paradise Lost* in 'The earth is all before me' (15), Wordsworth undermines Milton's implicit suggestion that Adam and Eve faced expulsion from the protection of Paradise with trepidation, 'The world was all before them, where to choose . . .' (*Paradise Lost* xii: 646). Instead of being 'scared' at liberty (16), Wordsworth *welcomes* the wilderness. The choice of a 'wandering cloud' (18) as guide is appropriate, first of all in that its dissolving form is part of a progressive dissolution of limits from the beginning to the end of the paragraph. Breeze, field, cloud, sky and water contrast with the severe geometry of the city walls (7). More specifically, though, the Exodus theme is continued in the image of God in the pillar of cloud that went before the tribes of Israel in their journey through the desert to the Promised Land (Exodus, 13, 21) – 'should the guide I chuse/Be nothing better than a wandering cloud/I cannot miss my way' (17–19). Wordsworth's journey, too, is conceived in terms of moving towards a paradise, so that we can detect from the outset his sense of being especially visited and guided. The 'gentle breeze' as 'messenger' and 'friend' recalls the Holy Spirit which took the form of a wind from heaven (Acts 2: 2), while the shaking off of his burden 'As by miraculous gift' (22) recalls how the chains of the imprisoned St Peter 'fell off from his hands' when the angel appeared (Acts 12: 6–7).

'I breathe again' (19) reintroduces the notion of unbridled freedom. The first 'word' of the paragraph, 'Oh', is itself an opening out, a breath, or non-verbal expression of feeling. It is a revolutionary way to begin an epic poem. *The Prelude* will constantly revaluate the function of words in this way. In Book III the Poet implies that his whole attempt at writing the poem is no more than to make 'Breathings for incommunicable powers' (III: 188). His entire mental state reflects the free upward movement from fields to sky, 'mountings of the mind' (20), in contrast with the downward depression of 'The heavy weight of many a weary day' (24). No intellectual effort breaks his almost existential state ('Trances of thought' (20)). The delightful prospect of 'Long months of ease and undisturbed delight' (28) leads him to pose further open questions (29–32). Now, the definite line of 'road or pathway' blurs into 'open field' (30) and finally into the capricious river-currents (31–2) which will point out a course which is without direction.

Lines 33–54

The mood changes here as we move from directionless freedom to 'chosen tasks' (34). Although these are 'chosen tasks' rather than obligations, 'dedicate myself to chosen tasks' marks a new commitment. What he hopes for now is work ('active days' (51)), a noble occupation (51–2), a high purpose, great achievements (53), amounting to a sanctified life (54). He does not exactly want to be a 'settler' (36), which has overtones of city-dwelling from which he has just escaped. He wants instead to pursue a kind of middle course ('drink wild water . . . pluck green herbs' (37)) between 'settling' on the one hand and 'tiresome' (35) lack of direction on the other. What in line 19 was felt as release, a natural breathing, now becomes a self-conscious and artful metaphor for poetic creation, an internal 'creative breeze' (43). The elaborate metaphor is one way in which a simple emotion is directed into conscious art. This breeze/breath metaphor is expanded into the storm images which follow. The 'mild creative breeze' (43) becomes a 'tempest' (46) so that the potential creativity he feels coming from within is excessive, 'redundant' (46). He has literally too much inspiration. Inspiration needs to be given a form or a channel into which it can be directed, but here it seems to elude direction, as though it threatens to destroy the few things it has made ('Vexing its own creation' (47)). Inspiration blowing free, then, is threatening, capricious, and wayward. We should notice, too, how the joy in the pastoral 'green fields' (2) becomes here, 'prowess in an honorable field' (52). The image has changed from a pastoral to an epic one since line 52 implies a battlefield. This transition from ease to a state of preparedness suggests that the life of verse (54) will involve strife. What form Wordsworth's work will actually take is still vague. Clearly, however, this paragraph attempts to organise the freedom of the previous one, and it is evident that his aspirations (53) will involve difficulties. The inspiration metaphor suggests that this new-found energy may actually thwart itself in its very struggle to find expression.

Lines 55–67

He now comments on the spontaneity of the previous lines, for his poetry ('measured strains' (57)) is more usually the product of emotion recollected in tranquillity, hence – 'not used to make/A present joy the matter of my song' (55–6). He had a feeling of being specially 'singled out' (62) for 'holy services' (63), and it was as though the spontaneous 'poetic numbers' (60) 'clothed' (61) his spirit in a 'priestly robe' (61). This image implies a kind of containment of that freedom which has been present from the beginning. The robe brings a new burden of responsibility, restraining the wayward impulse of the spirit. The last four lines (64–7) take up the issue of spontaneity (55–61). It is significant that a paragraph which begins with a consideration of 'present joy' (56) as a source of poetry, should end by qualifying this slightly. He was 'cheared' by spontaneous expression – 'My own voice' (64), but 'far more' (64) by 'the mind's/Internal echo of the imperfect sound' (64–5). It is the mental reverberations which matter almost more than the experiences themselves (see, for example, lines 417–26). The phrase 'Internal echo' (65) suggests a mental depth and space.

Lines 68–94

This paragraph returns from a passionate and immediate

[4]

engagement with a task to a mood more reminiscent of paragraph one. The emotions are too highly wrought to be sustained and so, 'not unwilling' (68), he now gives 'A respite to this passion' (69). There is a mood of gradual disengagement and a sinking back into relaxation. Pastoral calm succeeds excitement over epic possibilities. Like some classical shepherd he 'came erelong/To a green shady place where down I sate/Beneath a tree' (70–2). The disengagement was deliberate, 'slackening my thoughts by choice' (72), as though, having tested his capabilities, he now chose to rest up and luxuriate in a sheer contentment of mind and body. Bodily tension subsided but mental activity continued; 'On the ground I lay/Passing through many thoughts' (79–80). His thoughts about where he would live, what he would write, were preoccupying and brought on a mood of reverie. Meanwhile Nature's stillness encouraged this mood of relaxation, the earth became his 'pillow' (88), the grove of oaks his 'bed' (93), but it was also a ministry which nurtured him ('soothed', 'balanced' (89–90)) and finally startled him 'else lost/Entirely' (90–1) out of his musings.

Lines 95–115

Having already experienced the delight of inspiration he now tried to recover it, 'my soul/Did once again make trial of the strength/Restored to her afresh' (101–3). The paragraph deliberately recalls the first one with its unbidden delight in inspiration and its sense of freedom. Hence, 'bidding then/A farewell to the city left behind' (97–8), echoes 'from yon city's walls set free' (7); 'Even with the chance equipment of that hour' (99) recalls ' 'tis shaken off,/That burthen of my own unnatural self' (22–3). It is as though he was conscious of trying to re-create the initial situation. The difference is that this time, even with the presence of the breeze ('nor did she want/Eolian visitations' (103–4)) inspiration failed him. The image is a Romantic commonplace, the aeolian harp, where the poet became the strung harp from which the breeze of inspiration, sweeping across the strings, produced music (poetry).

The phrase 'slackening my thoughts by choice' (72) had implied a previous tautness in the strings. That he 'made trial' of his strength again suggests that he tautened them as before, only to find that, now, 'straggling sounds' (106) gave way to silence. For the time being, however, he was content to justify his lapse back into inactivity ('Be it so' (107)). Where previously he had called the creation of poetry 'holy' (63) he now says that to have other thoughts than ones of pure and simple 'present joy' (109) would be to 'bend the sabbath of that time/To a servile yoke' (112–13); in other words, it would be like desecrating the Sabbath on which we are commanded to refrain from servile works. So, first of all, it seemed, activity was 'holy', now, it seems, inactivity was holy. Entirely contradictory standards of holiness are being set up. Bending under the yoke reminds us of his being clothed in a priestly robe – as though a poetic vocation was seen as a kind of burden after all, something under which one might be expected to 'bend'. The 'servile yoke' reminds us of its opposite, 'enfranchised and at large' (9) where purposeless freedom had been like a liberation from slavery ('enfranchised'). The failure of inspiration, therefore, seems to produce a kind of rationalisation or even evasion of a problem which has emerged. Yet as Wordsworth lapses finally, even willingly, into inactivity again, there comes a hint of a new purposefulness. Now, instead of taking clouds as his guides and wandering aimlessly through open fields, he pursued a 'road' (110). He began to move towards his 'hermitage' (115) which possibly has overtones of the reclusive Milton's retirement prior to his writing *Paradise Lost*. The westering sun (96–7) implies a destiny (see e.g. *Stepping Westward*).[1] On the other hand, 'What need of many words?' (113) is a reminder of the restraints which language puts upon feeling, pure and simple. One part of him, therefore, appears to be saying that present joy (109) transcends definition or poetic expression. Another part suggests that directionless freedom is inadequate and needs to be channelled into a purpose. The rhythm of the paragraphing is organised in precisely this kind of way.

Lines 116–41

Now, in conformity with his belief that feeling should not be pressed into expression, he will 'spare to speak' (116) of what is self-sufficient, 'complete/Composure' and 'happiness entire' (121–2). But immediately ('speedily' (123)), in stark contrast, the longing to be more definite and to give himself to something purposeful returns. The relaxed mood of 'loitering' (114) and 'Composure' (122) is now replaced by 'bracing' (124), and 'Reading or thinking' (125) replaces 'What need of many words?' (113). There was a sense of urgency ('timely interference' (127)) in his original desire to give permanence to his experiences in a poem and so preserve them from 'decay' (126). He had intended to 'fix' these 'floating' mental images (129–31) and invest them moderately with his own feelings (132–3). Now, he finds that only gleams or flashes of inspiration are all he can achieve, and his frustration at being unable to create becomes the theme of the next few paragraphs.

Lines 142–56

Bracing, determination, and grappling are now replaced by yielding (142). His immediate contentment would be to abandon his ambitions for works of 'humbler industry' (144). He concentrates on his own imbalance where he is neither 'sick nor well' (147). The poet and the lover have the same 'fits' (147) (cp. 'The lunatic, the lover, and the poet/Are of imagination all compact' – *A Midsummer Night's Dream* V: i,7). There is a close analogy in Wordsworth's own lyric *Strange fits of Passion*[2] where, in the guise of a lover, he finds that his 'distress' is indeed the product of no more than his own 'Unmanageable thoughts' (149). The process of vacillating between 'brooding' (152) and 'goadings on' (153), as though restlessness is intrinsic to even the very symbol of peace itself (i.e. the mother dove (151)), is the pattern of life which Wordsworth traces throughout *The Prelude*. The poem progresses in terms of what he calls later 'Tumult and peace' (VI: 567), so that the contrary states in these first paragraphs are really providing a key to an understanding of the work as a whole.

Lines 157–228

Like Milton, preparing for *Paradise Lost*, he has made 'rigorous inquisition' (159) into his own capacities for undertaking 'such a glorious work' (158). Imagination, or the 'vital soul' (161) is his 'first great gift' (161) unlike what Dr Johnson, for example, saw as first in importance, namely 'general truths' (162).[3] For Johnson, depicting objective truths was the aim of every poet and the transforming powers of the living mind were merely decorative 'extras'. For Wordsworth here, Johnson's general truths have become secondary or 'Subordinate helpers of the living mind' (164). He refers to 'external things' (165) such as landscapes ('Forms, images' (166)) which help him as a poet but is vague about the 'numerous other aids' (166). The emphasis, however, on their being won with 'toil' (167) together with the 'rigorousness' of the self-inquisition brings the notion of effort and definite purpose back into prominence. The choice of an appropriate subject for the great poem becomes the main concern of the rest of the paragraph. Milton had said that *Paradise Lost* would be a poem that 'aftertimes . . . should not willingly let . . . die,'[4] but Wordsworth has no 'perfect confidence' (173) that he can make his own 'little band of yet remembered names . . . inmates in the hearts of men/Now living, or to live in times to come' (172/ 175–6). He considers subjects ranging from a tale of romance 'by Milton left unsung' (180) to tales of chivalry, and then loftier epic stories, all of which are similar in that their heroes were defenders of liberty. The long list ensuing enacts on a large scale Wordsworth's own divided impulses between freedom and restraint. The noble themes he seeks in tales of historic struggles for liberty are to be found in a great body of traditional epic whose very weight imposes a tremendous burden upon his freedom. There follows story after story of the noble dead. The ecstatic breathing in of freedom at the opening of Book I recedes ever further. When the 'soul/Of liberty' is mentioned now (195–6), it is linked to a phrase 'fifteen hundred years/Survived' (196–7), whose weight seems to deny the sense of liberty and brings in other notions of history and tradition instead. Later in the paragraph liberty is 'stern' (219). Wordsworth's attempt to escape from tradition by perhaps making up his own story for a poem (220ff.) meets only with 'deadening admonitions' (225). It is as though his duty lies in obeying the laws of the received epic, and as if writing this epic can only mean labouring under a terrible sense of responsibility.

Lines 228–71

His 'last wish' (228), to write a 'philosophic' poem (230), is expressed with passionate feeling ('I yearn towards . . .' (230)). But writing it would involve more mental effort than spontaneity, 'Thoughtfully fitted to the Orphean lyre' (234), and he shrinks from such an 'awful burthen' (235). He begins to suspect his own motives and suggests that his defaulting is a shirking of responsibility, 'I . . . /Take refuge, and beguile myself' (235–6). In the same way that morally confused people are unable to distinguish between right and wrong, he, too, is a living 'mockery' (239) or imitation of the almost inseparable 'brotherhood/Of vice and virtue' (239–40). He is unable in his confused state to distinguish between, first of all, the longing born of impotence and the longing which is healthy (240–2), or between timorousness and prudence, or between commendable circumspection and mere delay. He is in a state of moral confusion where he suspects that he is calling his actual selfishness 'Humility' or 'modest awe' (245) and can therefore no longer trust these things as virtues ('themselves/Betray me' (245–6)). This excessive scrupulousness may be only a selfish excuse for doing nothing and it paralyses his 'functions' (248) and 'beats off/Simplicity and self-presented truth' (250–1). The point here is that although he is having to make a tremendous struggle to reach it, *actual* truth, when it presents itself, is clear and simple. His thoughts return to freedom, 'Ah, better far than this to stray about/Voluptuously . . . given up/To

vacant musing, unreproved neglect' (252–5). He is thinking here
not of a reprehensible neglect but rather of a virtuous, almost
holy, abandonment of worldliness. He has all along been inter-
mittently dissatisfied with 'vacant musing' and is still unable to
find release in any firm commitment to his 'task' (260). The
resigned tone of 'This is my lot' (263) seems to bring the matter to
a conclusion. But further considerations ensue and accurately
convey the restlessness of his mind. He seeks 'repose' (267) *from*
'vain perplexity' in 'indolence' (268), a futile hope in itself. All
along he had felt that he was being singled out (62) for special
purposes. Now he feels like the false steward of the New
Testament (Matt. 25: 14–30) 'who hath much received/And
renders nothing back' (270–1). The process of being tossed from
one state of mind to another is brought to a resolution only by a
dramatic switch of direction. This crisis point is similar to the one
later, in Book X, when, describing his divided loyalties during the
French Revolution and 'wearied out with contrarieties', he
'Yielded up moral questions in despair' (899). His actual response
at that time was, as it is here, to change direction. He turned from
the complexities of man and society to the simplicities of Nature,
just as here he turns from his conflicting self to his simpler childhood self.

With the question 'Was it for this' (271) at the beginning of the
next paragraph, Wordsworth begins the history of his mind's
development from childhood. The poem as it goes on, therefore,
purports to be no more than an examination of what has brought
him as far as this crisis. 'Was it for this' is a crux marking the
collapse of epic ambitions into pastoral simplicity. It is a kind of
dead-end where he suddenly realises the misguidedness of trying
to find poetic fulfilment in traditional materials. Though all the
topics he mentioned reflect his predilection for liberty, none of
them is true to the strongest and earliest of his inspirations,
Nature. It is even as though the 'Impediments' (141) which stood
in his way when he would have gladly grappled with 'some noble
theme' (139) were being placed there by Nature herself, directing
him into her service as someone 'singled out' (62). The transition
at this point is not only from epic to pastoral but from the paralysis

of bewilderment to inspirational certainty. Wordsworth now equates the conventionally 'epic' with his own uncertainty and the pastoral mode with vigour and integrity. From the resonant histories of Mithridates, Sertorius, etc. we move to the gentle murmurings of the River Derwent and to the location of great things in small, *The Prelude*'s theme in a multitude of ways. So far the paragraphs have dramatised this paradox for us in terms of almost irreconcilable opposites. It is at this point that these opposites begin to cohere into a relationship.

Lines 271–304

From the disjointedness and internal division, therefore, emerges a new sense of harmony – the river 'loved/To blend his murmurs with my nurse's song' (272–3). The restless antithetical patterning which reflected the tortured mind is now replaced by a flow. Imperceptibly, the Derwent becomes the river of his mind. The 'voice/That flowed along my dreams' (275–6) is the first of several instances where mental travelling is likened to the course of a river. The 'murmurs' of the Derwent which introduce a passage of lyrical calm and beauty, answer the question Wordsworth had asked in the beginning, 'what sweet stream/Shall with its murmurs lull me to my rest?' (13–14). Musical imagery is employed. The 'ceaseless music' (279) of the stream had a 'steady cadence' (280) or rhythm, 'tempering' (280) his waywardness. The musical cadence of the stream 'composed' (281) his thoughts (made music of them). Where he had before struggled in vain to compose, we now find him passively composed (calmed). His 'more than infant softness' (282) is like that 'more than inland peace' of Furness Abbey later in Book II (115). We have become, by this stage, so merged into the peace of the remembered pastoral that the reasons for dismay have dwindled. The rest of the paragraph with its description of the child bathing returns us to that lovely sense of freedom at the beginning of the Book. The activities are all un-limited and unorganised, 'one long bathing' (294), 'coursed' (296), 'leaping' (297), 'wantonness' (303). The immersion in the stream

[11]

(295) is almost a baptism into the life of Nature. The child is the radical opposite of all that has gone before. Through him we pass out of the oppressive world of cultural tradition, a closed framework encouraging a sense of inadequacy, and into a world of total potential.

Lines 305–32

The organic nature of *The Prelude* or 'growth of a poet's mind' is reflected in the image of the 'seed-time' (305) of the soul. The sprouting seed was soon to be 'transplanted' (309) to Hawkshead, thirty or so miles from Cockermouth and the setting of the previous paragraph's adventures. The Poet was 'Fostered' (306) both by 'beauty' and by 'fear' (306) – that is, he was not only nurtured but also raised by them as substitute parents. His mother had, in fact, died in the previous year (1778), and his father, never a particularly intimate figure, was to die four years later. The slightly older child of almost 'Nine summers' (311) is presented as a different being from the 'five years' child' (291) in the last paragraph. Instead of being naked (292/304) he was now clothed, even armoured, 'my shoulder all with springes hung' (317) reminding us of how, previously, the innocent 'green fields' of line 2 had given way to 'prowess in an honorable field' (52). The boy was no more an infant partner of Nature's sharing in its innocence, but had become a 'fell' (cruel, ruthless) destroyer of it (318); perhaps, too, a destroyer of the Lakeland fells. A new 'adult' consciousness had replaced innocence. His 'anxious visitation' (320) to the snares was 'plied' (319), for example, like plying a trade. Instead of a physical, unthinking immersion (bathing and basking in water and sunshine) he was full of 'strong desire' (325), and his progress was 'hurrying' (321). At Cockermouth he had been identified with the river, but had now become more associated with the fretfulness of adulthood (283). His activities had been unrestricted and timeless but were now a 'hurrying' attempt to defeat time. Instead of being in rhythm with the day, part of the natural process of sunlight and flowing water, he was now out of rhythm (320–1) and he felt uneasy and self-conscious (322–4). Furthermore, the younger child was described in summer and in daylight, the older is described in winter and at night. The younger was under the sun, the older under 'Moon and stars' (321). Where the five-year-old's delight was to 'sport' (303) in the sense of play, the older child's sport was more destructive. The anxiety (320) in the woodcock episode prefigured his own 'over-anxious eye' (249) later in life. Wordsworth gives the passage a mock-heroic tone using gothic ingredients. The phrase 'and when the deed was done' (328) evokes the same kind of nameless horror we associate with Macbeth. That a small boy should have been a 'night-wanderer' (325) at all is obviously questionable, but Wordsworth's point is that it was only by ignoring the routine of childhood discipline that he could be receptive to magical impressions.

Lines 333–50

The passage of the seasons is unobtrusive. The five years' child belonged to summer. The 'last autumnal crocus' (313) took us from autumn to winter, and now we are returned to spring. Although the crocus was snapped by the frost and the primrose prematurely 'Decoyed' (335) by the sun, there was a purpose behind the destruction. The child, on the other hand, was a 'plunderer' (336) in springtime and a 'fell destroyer' (318) in winter. The destruction was purposeless, but Nature could turn even this to the child's own advantage, 'Though mean/My object and inglorious, yet the end/Was not ignoble' (339–41). As hunter he became himself the hunted. The hunting term 'Decoyed' describing the 'shining sun' (334) luring the primrose into flower, suggests in its context a benevolence behind the more usual destructive sense – a benevolence which was also shown to the boy. The 'knot of leaves' (334) from which the flower gently emerged looks forward to the stronger 'Knots of grass' (342) which supported the climbing boy. Although the ridge of rock was 'perilous' (347) he was 'sustained' (344) and 'Suspended' (345).

There is a sense in which the 'strange utterance' (348) of the wind, like the murmurings of the river (273), was an attempt at communication, an example of what he later calls 'the speaking face of earth and heaven' (V: 12). There is an abrupt drop from 'sky' (349) to 'earth' (350) and back to sky again ('clouds' (350)) so that the effect is to produce the boy's feeling of vertigo as he 'hung alone' (347).

Lines 351–71

Musical metaphors are reintroduced. The composition of the mind is the result of something like the invisible reordering processes of music which create harmony out of discord. This 'dark/Invisible workmanship' (352–3) 'reconciles' (353) the mind's 'Discordant elements' (354) and makes them harmonise. 'Regrets, vexations, lassitudes' (357) have been transformed into that 'calm existence' (360) which he recognises as his own when he is worthy of himself (361). The disharmony of the first part of the Book can now be seen as uncharacteristic and unworthy of him, and is here replaced by harmony. Although he is concerned with the 'means' (362) which Nature employed in fostering him, the poem as a whole looks forward to an 'end' (361). Wordsworth is, therefore, different from theorists like Burke (see the *Enquiry* 1756)[5] who were primarily interested in *what* was happening when emotions of fear or love were experienced. Wordsworth's concern is with the *value* of such emotions. He therefore gives 'Thanks' (362) for the means, but reserves his 'Praise' for the 'end' (361). A sense of being 'favored' (364) lies behind the lightning image. To be killed by lightning is, in a strange sort of way, to be specially singled out. Wordsworth was similarly sought out (366) but, in his case, with 'gentlest visitation' (367). We are reminded, too, of how the sun had sought gently for the primrose among its leaves. Although the flower may have been exposed to the chill of early spring by being 'Decoyed' (335), the purpose behind such processes was a wise one. In this way Wordsworth recognises that the 'Severer interventions' (370) 'dealt' (371) out to him had the 'selfsame end' (368) as her gentler visitations.

[14]

Lines 372–427

An example of severer interventions ('ministry/More palpable'
(370–1)) follows immediately. The boating episode took place in a
part of the Lake District which was unfamiliar (376–7), and therefore what happened to him was more likely because he was
unacquainted with the topography. A combination of solitude,
holiday freedom, and the lateness of the hour encouraged fantasy.
The landscape was typically transformed by his imagination into a
world of romance. His 'small skiff' (380) became an 'elfin pinnace'
(401) and went heaving through the water 'like a swan' (404)
leaving behind it a 'track/Of sparkling light' (393–4). He was
therefore primed to be affected in just the way he was by the huge
shape when it appeared. It was part of the faery world in which he
had become absorbed and strode after him like some fiend or giant
in a tale of romance. Running parallel with this intriguing recre-
ation of the child's experience is the mature Wordsworth's hand-
ling of the optical illusion which had worked upon him. Night and
moonlight had combined to bring about an alteration in natural
perspective. As the boy rowed out into the lake he 'fixed a steady
view' (397) upon the top of a mountain ridge which made up the
bound of his horizon. As he rowed further out, however, a more
distant peak rose up from behind the ridge. In daylight he would
have been able to see the dividing line between ridge and peak, but
the effect of moonlight was to obscure this detail. In fact, all he
saw was the first black silhouetted shape suddenly grow dramatically in bulk as he rowed away and seem to come towards him. At
this point, the world his imagination had created and the optical
illusion fed off each other. To make the shape get smaller he would
have to row *towards* it – the last thing he wanted to do. Instead he
'struck, and struck again' (408) which only made it get bigger. The
surprise of finding that what he rowed away from got bigger
instead of smaller filled him with panic because it seemed as
though a 'living thing' (411) was coming after him. At some point
he 'turned' (412), although he was very shaken, and was left only
with a sense of 'unknown modes of being' (420), of something
dark, unnameable, 'call it solitude' (421). It is as though naming is

inadequate ('call it solitude if you like'). More than anything he had a new sense of the mind as its own place. All the familiar world of sight, 'shapes' (422), 'images' (423), and 'colours' (424) deserted him, and what remained, whatever its nature, was something more adequately described in terms of what it was *not*. The phrasing is all absence and negation, 'blank desertion', 'no familiar shapes' (422), 'no colours' (424), 'forms that do not live/Like living men' (425–6). The experience left him with a new knowledge of the imagination's ability to create, as he says elsewhere, 'impressive effects out of simple elements' (Note to *The Thorn*, *Lyrical Ballads*, 1800).[6]

Lines 428–51

The poet suddenly assumes a solemn and prayer-like tone. It is a direct address, an elevated and impassioned thanksgiving, as if by a prophet or priest (see lines 59–63) to his god, 'Wisdom and spirit of the universe,/Thou soul . . .' (429). We are in the presence of immensities and yet attention is upon the utterly small, 'beatings of the heart' (441). The idea is of the small boy, his heart beating with fear, being somehow responsive to the 'grandeur' (441) and sublimity of the 'universe' (428), an elevation of little into grand. Something so negative as the 'pain and fear' (440) felt by the boy in the previous lines (372–427) is purified (437) and sanctified (439) until it grows into something greater – the very sentiment of wonder and awe which the mature poet expresses in this paragraph. Fear, we may say, is a primitive, elemental (438), religious emotion and, looking back, we can recognise this aspect of the boy's experience (416–20). In other words, the boy is not being punished for stealing. The fear does not serve as a correction or discipline. It is not a punishment, but a kind of privilege (a 'fellowship', 442). The 'discipline' (439) is nothing imposed upon the boy, but refers to the refining process which takes place when 'high objects' (436) – e.g. the mountain – impose their discipline upon fear itself. It develops into wonder (e.g. 419–20).

In these lines, there is no focus on the child's point of view. That was, quite literally, the focus in the previous lines (372–427). We move from a subjective viewpoint to an objective one. We are not enclosed within the dark confusions of the boy's mind, but are invited to consider the overall process, the development of pain and fear in the mind. The paragraph appeals to the intelligence of 'we' (440), the philosophic readers who, in our maturity, may be able to recognise a 'Wisdom' (428) where the boy could not. This 'Wisdom' intertwined (433) childish passions or feelings with 'high objects, with enduring things' (436), thus linking the insignificant to the vast. Note the tone of mature intelligence there from the paragraph's beginning. The line, 'Thou soul that art the eternity of thought' (429), means 'Thou soul to which human thought has given the (abstract and intellectual) term, eternity.'

The phrase 'trembling lake' (447) echoes the earlier phrase 'trembling hands' (412). An adjective referring to the boy's sensation of fear now refers to a movement in the lake (a sensation?), a pervading 'everlasting motion' (431). It is ambiguities such as this which subtly suggest the nature of the animate world. The boy's experiences were independent of the restrictions of time, taking place as they did 'both day and night' (450) and 'all the summer long' (451).

Lines 452–73

The constraints of time and of society emerge very clearly, however, at the beginning of this paragraph. In the 'Clear and loud' (457) sound of the striking clock and in the 'summons' (455) of the lighted cottage windows there is an implication that the duty of children was to avoid idle pursuits and to retire to bed early in order to be more diligent and industrious on the morrow. Wordsworth ignored this summons by a deliberate turning away, 'I wheeled about' (458). There is a deliberately challenging use of the phrase 'not . . . idle' (466), referring to the happy voices of children at play. Such 'idleness' was a fulfilment and the emotive word is given a positive meaning.

Freedom from constraint is implicit in the image of the horse

(459), (cp. 'I unloosed her tether' (382)) leading on to a comparison of the skating boys ('shod with steel' (460)) to huntsmen (462–4). The effect of the boating passage had depended on the visual sense, whereas this skating episode is mainly auditory, 'resounding' (463), 'bellowing' (464), 'din' (466), 'rang' (467), 'Tinkled' (469). In this emphasis upon the two primary senses of eye and ear we can see a definite order in the presentation of the paragraphs.

In spite of the gaiety and almost anarchic pleasure described here, there is an unobtrusive sadness which is disturbing. The village clock 'tolled' (458), the distant hills sent 'an alien sound/Of melancholy' (470–1), and the orange sky of evening 'died away' (473). The young Wordsworth's tangential sense of this, present in 'not unnoticed' (471), can be linked to his dim awareness of something just over the edge of consciousness, expressed in liminal words like 'dawn' (432) and 'margin' (447) in the previous paragraph, 'twilight' (454) in this one, 'shadowy' (480) in the next. The 'lonely scene' (445), 'gloomy hills' (448), 'alien sound' (470) add to the sense of 'unknown modes of being' (420), resisting familiarity yet somehow too present to be entirely disregarded.

Lines 474–89

In the last paragraph Wordsworth tells us that the intensity of his personal feeling was greater than that of his playfellows – 'happy time/It was indeed for all of us, to me/It was a time of rapture' (455–7). In this we see him physically separate himself from them to pursue his own activities which had, in turn, a deeper awareness. This private withdrawal seems to happen on three occasions. First of all in a kind of youthful seeking out of solitude ('Into a silent bay' (475)), then 'sportively' (475) chasing a star, and finally in what begins communally, 'And oftentimes/When we . . .' (478–9) but ends in solitude, 'Have I . . .' (483).

Noise ('uproar' (474) and 'tumultuous' (476)) faded away as the resistless presence of the 'silent bay' (475) seemed to kill off all thought of joy and frivolity. The predominant tone at the end of

the paragraph is 'solemn' (487). The boy went in the straight line
of a speed-skater, rapidly, like a fishing-line running off a reel
('spinning still/The rapid line of motion' (481–2)). There would
probably be no clearer example in Wordsworth's time (as there are
many in our own) of such high-speed dynamics. The phraseology
needs to be carefully read. It is the 'shadowy banks' (480) which
sweep through the darkness as he raced past them. It is the skater
who spins the rapid line ('spinning still/The rapid line . . ./Have
I . . ./Stopped short' (481–4)). Stopped short does not mean that
he came to a full stop. It means that he ceased to propel himself,
got down from the erect position on to his heels, and continued to
speed along, gradually losing momentum as he glided to a standstill. Just as in the boating episode the boy's movement alone made
the mountain seem to move, so here it is only the skater's speed
which had the effect of making the cliffs go round (484–5). The
phenomenon, perhaps best seen from the window of a moving
train, is of the speeding foreground and more slowly moving
background turning away from the observer on a common pivot,
like a roundabout turns away when one stands at its edge. The
slowly turning cliffs produced exactly the same effect, and it was
as though ('even as if' (485)) he could actually see the world
turning slowly in its daily ('diurnal') revolution. Of course, as he
glided to a standstill the apparent turning movement 'on either
side' (480) became 'Feebler and feebler' (488) and eventually
stopped when he did. There is a precise awareness on the Poet's
part of astronomical ('diurnal') and scientific law in this passage.
The same laws which produced the turning effect were also at
work in the pursuit of the reflected star. The 1850 version makes it
clearer . . . 'leaving the tumultuous throng,/To cut across the
reflex of a star/That fled, and, flying still before me, gleamed/
Upon the glassy plain' (I, 449–52). 'I stood and watched' (488),
the next thing he did, is characteristic of his fixed observation.
There are similar phrases elsewhere, such as 'I gazed – and gazed'
('Daffodils'). Both this paragraph and the last one make us aware
of the orbital and cyclical processes of the universe, the world
itself, and the seasons; 'wheeled' (458/485), 'spinning' (481),
'rolled' (485), have obvious turning meanings, whereas 'Eastward

. . . west' (472) and the word 'diurnal' (486) itself (contrast 'daily'), less obvious ones. Less obtrusive still is the way in which Wordsworth has taken us through a complete cycle of seasons – from summer (296ff.), to autumn and winter ('The frost . . . had snapped/The last autumnal crocus' (312–13)) through to 'spring-time' (333), and summer again (probably summer 'holidays' (378)), and now back to winter, 'And in the frosty season' (452). Whatever techniques the skating episode employs, however, we should not miss its sense of rapture. The Poet asks us simply to imagine the childhood scene – tiny figures hurling themselves about on an enormous plain of ice beneath a dark starry sky. The first of the two paragraphs depicts the boy wheeling and turning, the second the Universe doing the same thing. Just as, elsewhere, his heart 'dances with the daffodils' it is as though, here, boy and Universe are involved together in a giddy ecstatic dance, physical, abandoned ('given our bodies to the wind' (479)), and essentially non-rational.

Lines 490–501

The language takes on an elemental simplicity in phrases like 'in the sky' (490) and 'on the earth' (491). The 'presences' are not vague personifications but real forces at work. The prophetic voice of the Poet, 'Ye presences . . . ye visions' (490–1) gives the verse an elevated tone contrasting with the lowly 'vulgar hope' (493) which is dismissed. Wordsworth cannot be certain that Nature was active on his behalf, but the rhetorical function of 'can I think/A vulgar hope was yours when ye employed/Such ministry' (492–4) re-enforces the unlikelihood of such presences being meaningless or commonplace. They followed or sur-rounded (haunted) him (495), and animated all natural objects. Danger and desire became inseparable, 'delight' and 'fear' (500) mutually supportive. The whole regular 'surface of the universal earth' (499) was imbued with life and worked (fermented) 'like a sea' (501). The final lines are instinct with movement, so that the transformation of one element into another (solid earth to sea) is done in terms of a rhythm where the sea's waves can almost be visualised, 'With triumph, and delight, and hope, and fear' (500). In this line the flatness of 'surface' is broken into waves.

Lines 501–24

In his Preface to *The Excursion* Wordsworth had written that if, together with the elevated subject-matter of his poem *The Recluse*, he were to '. . . describe the Mind and Man/ Contemplating; and who, and what he was –/The transitory Being that beheld/This vision . . .' this labour would not be 'useless' (95–9).[7] Similarly here, in the process of describing that 'transitory Being', he talks of being not 'uselessly employed' (501). He reacts against the idea that poetry should be 'useful'. Earlier as we have seen, he had searched for high topics as his subjects, but the epic tradition had been a burden upon him. Here the subject sits lightly and is full of limitless possibilities. 'I might pursue this theme through every change/Of exercise and play to which the year/Did summon us in its delightful round' (502–4). The two activities he singles out, fishing and kite-flying, are related in so far as both connect the individual to the elements by means of a line. Both enable him to partake in Nature's very being (water and sky) but *not* to control it. The 'rod and line' (511) is a 'True symbol of the foolishness of hope' (512) while the kite, for no apparent reason, 'Dashed headlong and rejected by the storm' (524) suggests the capriciousness of a natural order which can promote or destroy at random. Although he felt himself specially favoured by Nature, he could not presume on her intercession, as tentative statements like, 'Surely I was led by her' (372) or the puzzling rejection of his kite imply. Fishing and kite-flying dealt with elemental forces which could not be controlled and the pleasure derived from them depended on this very unpredictability.

Lines 525–70

The prophetic voice opens this paragraph. Whereas it had opened the last but one with an address to immensities, 'Ye presences of Nature, in the sky/Or on the earth, ye visions of the hills . . .' (490–1) etc., here, the voice addresses 'lowly cottages' (525), themselves a contrast with the *soaring* kite of the last paragraph. Wordsworth gives this form of address to lowly things in order to heighten their importance. The descent to the 'lowly' is really a positive way of elevating the insignificant. Like Nature's 'ministry', the cottages too had 'a ministration' (526) of their own. They communicated a sense of caring and of belonging, 'A sanctity, a safeguard, and a love' (527). Their 'plain and seemly' (531) existence is the *reason* they are remembered. To have forgotten them would be an indication of moral deficiency, hence the rhetorical questions which imply how unthinkable this is. Behind the seemliness, however, lurked real passion and excitement, so that the plain appearances were deceptive (532–3). The children's pencil games 'With crosses and with cyphers scribbled o'er' at which they 'schemed and puzzled, head opposed to head' (538–9) sets elaborate difficulty indoors against the large uncomplications of Nature outside (562ff.). The effect is mildly humorous. The puzzling efforts of the child prefigure the problems of the adult Wordsworth at the beginning of the Book. His statement that such childish 'strife' is 'too humble to be named in verse' (540) is ironic in that this is exactly what he *has* done, while the game of cards described as though it were a battle ('strife') reminds us of how the epic mode is being handled. Warfare is a traditional epic subject, but Wordsworth is writing what might be called a pastoral epic. We are meant to see that the time-honoured theme, in so far as it is present at all, has been reduced to a game of cards played by children in a cottage. Just as the lowly cottages cared for (527) their inmates, so too the humble pack of cards was cared for by the children. The imagery makes us think of the cards as warriors. The pack is 'sent into battle' time and time again. But individual cards, although past their best, were not, like *real* discharged veterans, 'ungratefully thrown by' (545). Instead, they

[22]

were nurtured (Wordsworth uses a *pastoral* term, 'husbanded' 547) and preserved. The epic mode is employed but the destructive element of the 'long campaign' (547) is replaced by the fostering, promoting benefits which the pastoral celebrates. The 'plebean cards' (549) used as substitutes for missing Kings and Queens and therefore 'glorified' (551) and raised up 'beyond the promise of their birth' (550), is, in the implied wider context of the times, politically subversive, but clearly connected to the entire way in which, not only this paragraph, but much of Wordsworth's poetry takes humble and rustic life and raises it above the accepted norms and conventions of poetic subject material. Strictly speaking this passage is not, like the card game in Pope's *Rape of the Lock* from which it derives, mock-epic.[8] The mock-epic takes a lowly theme and makes it more *obviously* lowly or trivial by talking about it as though it were lofty. The point of this paragraph, however, is that the virtues of the lowly are in fact *elevated* above accepted standards of greatness. What is high and what is low change places so that we are invited to consider how we define the elevated. It is more true of this paragraph to call it 'Romance' than 'Mock-Epic'. Wordsworth again depicts himself as a born romancer. Just as in the boating episode he had created his own imaginary world, so here he weaves stories of myth and romance into a game of cards and makes the natural sounds of the moving ice into the 'dismal yellings' (569) of wolves, or a 'Bothnic main' (570) out of Lake Esthwaite. As in other early experiences he mentions, he was only peripherally aware of Nature. What was important were the immediate occupations such as skating or, as here, indoor games.

Lines 571–85

He begins this paragraph by saying how he has been careful ('sedulous') to 'trace' the ways in which Nature arranged that external activities passionately pursued ('extrinsic passion' (572)) caused him to become gradually aware of 'beauteous forms or grand' (573) for themselves only. In other words, skating, for example, may have been one of the passions of his youth, but the beautiful scenery in which he skated made a subliminal impression on his mind. It was later to become important for him when the 'passion' for skating had perhaps diminished. Even in these 'tempestuous' (577) times of childhood delight he had often felt a spiritual pleasure ('An intellectual charm' (580)) in the simple enjoyments of the senses (578). He attributes these 'joys/Of subtler origin' (575–6), as he calls them (i.e. subtler than the sensual activities themselves), to the instinctual affections ('affinities' (582)) for our natural habitat with which we are born. We find ourselves, as he says elsewhere, 'exquisitely . . . fitted' to the external world (*Preface to The Excursion* 64–6).[9] Here, these affections 'fit/Our new existence to existing things' (582–3) so that a close connection ('bond of union' (585)) to them inevitably promotes our joy. Notice the tentativeness with which he continues to make his statements, however, – 'that calm delight/Which, if I err not, surely must belong . . .' (580–1). To explore the 'Mind of Man' is indeed, as he says elsewhere, to 'tread on shadowy ground' (see *Preface to The Excursion* 28–40).[10] Nothing can be stated as factual, only intuited. The processes of Nature can only be 'traced' (571).

Lines 586–608

'Yes, I remember . . .' (586) is an affirmed recognition of those recalled 'pure motions of the sense' (578) at work. The images are sensory, not intellectual. The seasons, for example, stamp (587) their *impressions* on his mind; 'even then,/A child' (588–9) reminds us of the ability of the lowly stage of life to achieve unconsciously (589) what has only been understood with effort in adulthood. For Wordsworth, as for the seventeenth- and eighteenth-century sensationalist philosophers like Locke and Hartley, all mental experience is grounded in the senses.[11] Drinking is a primal experience, the first active sensation of infancy, and 'drinking in/A pure organic pleasure from the lines/Of curling mist' (590–2) means that he received the simplest of bodily ('organic') delights, uncomplicated by any thoughtfulness ('unconscious intercourse' (589)). His emotions at that time were intensely private, though known, he suggests, to the 'sands . . . creeks and bays' (594) which were involved in them ('they can tell') but not to other living beings.

As the sea gradually filled with light from the rising moon he would stand 'Engrafted in the tenderness of thought' (600), that is, incorporated fully within the 'intellectual charm' (580) that he has identified as part of primal sense experience. 'Engrafted in' has overtones of the intrinsic (what was going on inside) rather than those passions (e.g. skating) which he calls 'extrinsic' (572). Such moments were ones of primary sensation. They did not, in those early days, have associations with other similar remembrances ('linking with the spectacle/No conscious memory of a kindred sight' (601–2)) as the philosopher David Hartley had claimed inevitably happened as primary sensations were mechanically built upon by more complex ones throughout life. Nor did they find him already especially predisposed to 'quietness or peace' (604). That the light on the sea seemed to be giving 'sweet notice of the rising moon' (598) to the shepherds' huts is the pleasant notion of a mature poet, but 'to fancies such as these' in those primary stages of simple sensation he was 'A stranger' (601). Just as his primitive function was to 'drink' the beauty he saw, so too his eye gathered light – the most primitive of impressions. The landscape dissolved into light. The 'three long leagues/Of shining water' (605–6) – a 'field of light' (607), almost Turnerian in its effect, suggests no obstacle but rather limitless vistas, such as those with which Book I begins. Light was the first creation ('let there be light') and therefore pre-dates shape and form. Wordsworth intends to show that the young child's experiences were very basic ones – sensory, primitive, and unrestricted. His eye moved over the shining water taking minute pleasure in every 'hair-breadth' (607) of light like a bee sips nectar as it moves from flower to flower. The image combines ideas such as the smallness of the boy and immensity of his surroundings, the precision of his pleasure-gathering ('hair-breadth') and the vagueness of the light-field, with the overall notion of his freedom and intoxication with beauty.

Lines 609–40

The 'fits of vulgar joy' (609) and the 'tempest' (612) of 'giddy bliss' (611) contrast with the slow opening up of the large reaches towards infinity described in the previous paragraph. The 'vulgar joy' is the kind associated with superficial sports and pastimes and is 'prompt' (611) to attend such 'pursuits' (610). The other 'joys/ Of subtler origin' (575–6) are not tempestuous but 'calm' (580) and slower to haunt him. The slower proceedings are *emphatically* recalled – 'Yes, I remember' (586) but the 'prompt attendants' (611) are just as promptly 'forgotten' (613). That a feeling of 'bliss' (611), could work 'along the blood' (612) as though it were capable of physically affecting the senses shows how deeply rooted Wordsworth's most elevated moods were in the world of sense. 'I felt/Gleams' (613–14) involves two different senses (synaesthesia) as also does the image of 'drinking in' pleasure from something seen, 'the lines/Of curling mist' in the previous paragraph (590–2).

The language continues throughout to be sensationalist in the tradition of the philosopher David Hartley. The 'collisions' and 'accidents' here (617) were primary sensations and refer to the simple ones felt during boyhood sports and activities when mountains and lakes, etc., as we have seen, 'impressed' (620) themselves (in the Hartleian sense) indirectly upon his mind. At the time these sports or vulgar joys (625) were the most important things to him, and the scenes 'which were a witness of that joy' (627), that is, the beautiful landscapes, only secondary and peripherally attached ('Collateral' (621)) to them. He was brought into contact with them only, as it were, by 'chance collisions' (617), like the way in which incompatible people were once thought to have been made to fall in love by 'fairies' (619) (cp. Bottom and Titania in *A Midsummer Night's Dream*). Natural beauties were not, however, 'vain/Nor profitless' (619–20) if 'haply' (by chance) (620) they remained 'Depicted on the brain' (629) when the 'vulgar joy' (625) had been forgotten. As in the theory of the association of ideas, simple sensations 'frequently repeated' (633) amongst natural scenes provoked more complex ones until *ideas* of

Nature's beauty, the product of those sensations and therefore 'representative/Of joys that were forgotten' (634–5), became 'habitually dear' (638) and 'Allied to the affections' (640). Wordsworth, reflecting this theory, strives for a definition of what can be briefly summarised. The boyhood sports, often played out amongst lovely scenery, left important impressions of that scenery in the mind when the sports themselves were no longer pursued. But the complexity of the paragraph is of more value than a paraphrase and has its own point. There is a fluid sense of Wordsworth grappling with the process of elusive mental events, pursuing them through a labyrinth of qualifying sub-clauses until the final tying down in line 640 (the 1850 version has 'fastened' instead of 'allied'). The paragraph really falls into two halves, lines 609–24, and 625 to the end. The second half says substantially the same thing but in such a way as to suggest that Wordsworth is trying, even in the process of writing, to get things right – to clarify the issue for himself. The 'obscure feelings' (634) left as 'representative/Of joys that were forgotten' (634–5) are even more tenuous than the joys themselves, but the fragility is only apparent and words such as 'impressed' (620), 'substantial' (628), 'Depicted' (629), 'impressive' (631), 'force' (633), and 'links' (639) suggest the strength of the 'affections' (640) being formed. Similarly, the apparent hap-hazardness of events ('chance collisions' (617) '. . . if haply they impressed . . .' (620)) can be seen in retrospect to be part of that *purposeful* 'dark/Invisible workmanship' (352–3) building, directing, intertwining. The 'quaint accidents' (617) such as 'evil-minded fairies' (619) are supposed to cause are introduced, therefore, only to be rejected because in Wordsworth's case these chance collisions were not destructive but fostering and purposive. The mature mind was given life ('impregnated' (624)) by what had seemed 'lifeless' (622) and was elevated (624) by the very scenes which had, once, only been a backdrop to more obvious vulgar pleasures. The passage is not really about recall so much as it is about forgetting ('forgotten . . . Wearied itself out of the memory . . . joys that were forgotten' (613/26/35)). Wordsworth's interest is less in what he remembers than in what lies half-way between remembering and forgetting, and especially in the *processes* of this state of half-consciousness.

Lines 640–63

The paragraph opens with a kind of special pleading. He hopes he might be excused for indulging himself in memories which are no help in pushing ahead with the planned 'work/Of glory' (85–6). High adult purpose disowns such unreliable memories. He cannot even be certain that the memories have reality. He might have been imagining snowdrops (memories) when there was only really snow, a cold white absence of any life at all (643–4). But here the Poet's apologetic 'I fear' (641), and what he calls the 'weakness of a human love' (642) for his recollections, brings in a humble, gentle, and intimate tone, especially noticeable after the very intellectual previous paragraph. We are being asked now to respond to his memories with our hearts, not our heads, and to allow him his little 'weakness' as the sympathetic human beings he hopes we are, and as he hopes Coleridge is ('my friend' (645)). The promptness of Coleridge's sympathy (645–6) is gently elicited, 'Nor will it seem to thee . . . that I have lengthened out . . . a tedious tale' (645–7). The apologetic tone is deliberately rhetorical, however. Not for one moment does Wordsworth believe that his tale is 'fond and feeble' (647), and he invites us to make the right response. Only if we *do* make this response will we be able to see that the seemingly insignificant is being given more importance than the spurs of manhood and its 'honorable toil' (652–3). What probably prompts Wordsworth to make us question his 'spur-rings' are Milton's lines from *Lycidas*, 'Fame is the spur that the clear spirit doth raise . . . To scorn delights, and live laborious days.' The 'honorable toil' (653) is writing the epic which imposed an enormous burden of tradition upon him (157ff.), whereas here, the apparently irresponsible, the non-laborious and self-indulgent recollections are seen as being supportive to such an enterprise. Those things which seem weak, the 'snowdrops' (644) of memory, the 'fond' (foolish/sentimental) and the 'feeble' (647)

[28]

enable him to be strong, to 'fix the wavering balance' (650) of his mind – that is, the indecisiveness which was causing him to oscillate between periods of unlimiting freedom and the need to commit himself to a task.

Instead of spurring on, however, Wordsworth pauses in his recollections only to resume his journey *back*. He adopts a very half-hearted attitude to the 'honorable toil'. He might, he says ('haply' (651)) 'meet reproaches' which would goad him to his purpose, but, instead of 'shunning delights' in the high Miltonic fashion, he feels just the opposite inclination, 'loth to quit/Those recollected hours that have the charm/Of visionary things, and lovely forms/And Sweet sensations . . .' (658–61). It is as though to write about his past is to be charmed, detained, in a kind of pleasurable indolence and dalliance which he is reluctant to leave. And again, Coleridge and the reader are invited to be as weak as him and to comply with his self-indulgence, 'nor . . . need I dread from thee/Harsh judgments . . .' (655–8). The sprinkling of words like, 'fond', 'feeble', 'lovely', 'sweet', 'charm', suggests weakness but is in reality, a test of our strength of response. We ourselves would be weak if we failed to see that as *Wordsworth* is using them they are not weak words. Book I, therefore, does not go forward. It is concerned with those 'sweet sensations, that throw back our life' (661). Perhaps the retracing of steps made Wordsworth think of Orpheus ('Orphean lyre' (234)), prominently figured in *Lycidas*, and maybe in his mind at the beginning of Book II, 'Thus far . . . have we, though leaving much/Unvisited, endeavoured to retrace/My life through its first years, and measured back/The way I travelled . . .' (1–4).

Lines 664–74

His way forward is now to retrace his steps. The original end product which he had proposed to himself in the shape of a 'work/Of glory' (85–6) has been replaced by this much more pre-occupying history of his mind. As though to recall his earlier intention he writes that at least 'One end . . . hath been attained'

(664). By relaxing his intense pursuit of a subject and its attendant anxieties he has revived his mind (665) and the initial sense of limitless possibilities has been restored. Another echo of Milton, 'The road lies plain before me' (668; cp. 15), leads on to the interesting thought that just as the road before him really lies *behind*, so this new theme of his own life will not be 'Single and of determined bounds' (669) at all. It will be an exploration of the shadowy boundless territory of his mind. The 'ampler or more varied argument' (671) which it replaces was ironically the very one which was setting limits and imposing its burden upon him. His new 'labour' will therefore be 'welcome' (674) and will, in fact, be no labour, unlike the 'laborious days' which spur on to fame in *Lycidas*. At one stroke Wordsworth fixes the 'wavering balance' (650) of his mind. The total freedom of the beginning of the Book, and his compulsion to leave that freedom for a noble task become one. Writing *The Prelude* will now be his task, but it will also be a liberation.

Pattern of thought

Wordsworth recalls an earlier ecstatic mood of liberation and creative potential which has since, apparently, deserted him. A vacillating state of mind succeeds this mood of optimism whereby he is torn between relaxation in a kind of existential inertia on the one hand, and frustration at being unable to exploit his sense of great poetic gifts on the other. These two opposing inclinations reduce him to an agony of indecision, so that his mental paralysis can only be released by a radical lateral shift. Instead of committing himself to a poem on some lofty theme, deadening in its weight of received epic tradition and therefore at odds with the light, freeing mode of the opening 'song', Wordsworth goes back to examine how he received those very gifts which he believes have equipped him for poetic utterance. The poem which follows – *The Prelude* – begins as a statement about how Wordsworth is unable to write the intended work, and about how he has come to fall short of the promise held out to him.

The lateral shift in line 271, 'Was it for this . . .', turns attention to childhood not only as the origin of personality, but as a source of power and strength which rebukes his present weakness. Paradoxically, in searching for a subject large enough to do justice to his sense of inspiration and poetic ability, Wordsworth discovers not high epic but the insignificant playtime of his own infancy. What may seem diminutive and mean in his childhood experiences, however, is insistently related to what is disturbing, exciting and grandiose. Such experiences were a species of encounter with a god-like, universal spirit, so that the boy felt haunted, pursued, and terrified. We have a sense of the little child being somehow gathered up into the vast life of the universe, so that the lowly and humble are given high status. The poet can now see the apparently purposeless activities of childhood as moving towards a high purpose. Even idleness was profitable. The retracing of steps becomes Wordsworth's way forward and *The Prelude*, in consequence, the very work he was seeking to write. The antithesis of freedom and purpose at the beginning of the Book is, therefore, reconciled in a final synthesis.

BOOK II

Lines 1–47

Wordsworth makes clear, in his opening address to Coleridge ('Thus far, O friend, have we . . .'), that the spirit of this Book is not one of lonely reminiscence. Coleridge is a companion on the journey back through memory. So later is the whole crowd of childhood friends. 'And be ye happy! Yet, my friends, I know/ That more than one of you will think with me' (42–3). A mood of companionship and relationship, amounting to a 'great social principle of life' (408), goes right through the Book.

Going back over his past has been like a journey – 'leaving much/Unvisited' (1–2). The companions retrace the steps of a second journey, that of his life – 'The way I travelled when I first began/To love the woods and fields' (4–5). This love, only as yet 'in its birth' (6), was nourished quite by chance as an incidental effect of outdoor games (9). The children's world consisted of 'loud uproar' (15) and energetic play. The phrase 'round of tumult' (9) suggests a circular motion of time, no progression. There were, of course, moments of calm at bedtime when, in the quiet sky, 'the huge clouds/Were edged with twinkling stars' (16–17), but there was no inward reflection – only 'weary joints' and 'a beating mind' (18). The mind pulsed and throbbed with pleasant exhaustion, no wearisome thinking. The heedless play of

[32]

the children delighted the older onlookers watching on chairs, benches and threshold steps (11–12). We have a definite sense of community. Old and young, in particular, co-existed effortlessly. The old man, 'A later lingerer' (14) watched longest. Later, the old dame sold her wares near the grey stone which was also 'home/ And centre of these joys' (the games: 35–6). This is the paradise world to which we eventually return in Book VIII where, at Grasmere Fair, 'gaiety prevails/Which all partake of, young and old' (VIII: 45–6).

In the adult world as a whole, however, 'virtue' and 'intellect' (21) – not innocence or play – tend to be held up as matters of 'pride'. But, Wordsworth asks, do we not still hope for a child-like 'eagerness' (26) in moral and intellectual life? This is, in a way, he admits, to hope 'For things which cannot be' (24), a return to what is lost forever, but Wordsworth's childhood does repeatedly return across the wide 'vacancy' (29) of time. Youth, through memory, attends upon age. Though irretrievably apart in one sense, youth and age, (as in the living community), can come together. 'A tranquillising spirit' (27), an overwhelming silence or peace, suddenly seems to overcome him like an active force. It 'presses now' (27), as he writes, with the immediacy of physical sensation – 'On my corporeal frame' (28). In an intense hush of pure reflection, the mind observes its own workings. We focus not upon the past, but upon the *process* of remembering it. This process involves a strange paradox, of having the past self ('some other being' (33)) in the mind now, as a 'self-presence' (30). 'When I think of them' (those days) 'I seem/Two consciousnesses' (31–2). Again and again, there are pauses in the poem, when the Poet (as he writes) focuses attention upon his present self. We are let in on the experience and sensations of creation and composition.

We plunge back into the past. The 'grey stone/Of native rock' (33–4) was more than just a stone. It was a 'centre' (36) for the children, a trading post for the old dame. When, returning in later years, he found it 'split' (38), he suffered a rude shock of outrage. This comes out in the language used to describe its replacement, the 'assembly-room' (39). It was offensively 'smart' (39); it 'perked and flared/With wash and rough-cast' (39–40). In his

Guide to the Lakes, Wordsworth further expressed his distaste for the 'glare of whitewash'. He felt that houses should 'harmonize with the surrounding landscape'. Rough-cast he deplored because it 'has tended greatly to injure English landscape, and the neighbourhood of these Lakes especially, by furnishing such apt occasion for whitening buildings'.[1] The word 'perked' (39) conveys not only appearance, but a sense of impudence and unpleasant self-conceit. To split the stone was an act of disrespect for the old dame ('From whom the stone was named' (45)) and for the traditional customs of an old community. The dame had sold her wares at the stone 'through the length of sixty years' (47). Compared to the established community, the 'assembly-room' houses an assembly that is not an assembly at all. The phrase itself ('assembly-room') is thus ironic. The phrase 'elbowing the ground' (40) suggests a modern aggressiveness. The screaming fiddle (41) is discordant, shrill; it replaces the simple 'revelry' (14) of the children. Gone was the closeness of old and young, the old dame presiding over the games, the young accepting her without thought in unforced neighbourliness. The community of his youth did not need such artificial organising. Wordsworth, resigned, consoles himself that memory (or rather a community of memory (43)) will help to heal the sense of loss.

The point of this episode, then, is that Wordsworth does not regret the 'vacancy' between youth and age. It is simply inevitable that children and adults are apart – as the 1850 version puts it, there is a 'Union that cannot be' (24). Yet this first paragraph shows that there was a togetherness in the apartness – a community of spirit which the modern assembly-room denies. The situation is common in Wordsworth's poetry – old age and youth are often seen to be mutually supportive.

> The oldest and youngest
> Are at work with the strongest.

> ('Written in March')[2]

> We talked with open heart, and tongue
> Affectionate and true,

A pair of friends, though I was young,
And Matthew seventy-two.

('The Fountain')[3]

In the same way, old and young form a harmonious community in
William Blake's 'Ecchoing Green' (*Songs of Innocence*).

Old John with white hair
Does laugh away care,
Sitting under the oak,
Among the old folk.
They laugh at our play,
And soon they all say,
Such such were the joys
When we all girls & boys,
In our youth time were seen
On the Ecchoing Green.

Lines 48–78

The phrase 'the year span round' (48) implies both speed and
stillness in time's movement, like 'round of tumult' (9). The boy
was 'giddy' (49) and thoughtless of time's passage, but we are
aware of it. Now especially a new 'time approached' (49), when
'calmer pleasures' (51) balanced 'holiday delight' (53). An
important intermediate stage was now reached in the part played
in his life by boyish sports. Hitherto, they had been sought for
their own sake. Now the actual enjoyment of them depended
upon the presence of Nature's 'beauteous forms' (51). These latter
were 'collaterally attached' (52) to the sports, so that without this
beauty the sports would be only 'languidly pursued' (55). In the
next few lines 'calmer pleasures' (51) predominate over 'holiday
delight' (53).

Here, Nature's 'beauteous forms' were three islands, each with
its uniquely individual beauty, almost a rarefied magic. The birds'
music on the first seemed timeless; they 'sang forever' (60). The

'umbrageous covert' (61) of the second, and the carpet of flowers (62) intensify the feeling that these were little paradises – specially protected enclaves. The third brings a suggestion of continuity with the old dame and her stone table. Here, a hermit had also possessed 'An old stone table' (64). The phrase 'mouldered cave' (64) implies a gentle melancholy, a sweet sense of the past in contrast to everything that the smart new assembly-room made him feel. Most important was the effect of all this beauty, and this was to tone down 'jealousy' (67), 'pride of strength' (69) and 'the vainglory of superior skill' (70). Nature's beauty, that is, taught a moral lesson. 'We rested in the shade, all pleased alike' (68) describes a paradise replacing the war-like (if mock-heroic) tone of 'Conquered and conqueror' (69). Pastoral replaces epic (compare Book I: 525–70). Unpleasant competitiveness or 'pride of strength' (69) – as in the boating incident of Book I as well – were 'subdued' (71) and 'tempered' (72). An even quieter mood, almost a retreat, followed – described in the phrases 'A quiet independence of the heart' (73) and 'diffidence and modesty' (76). This is a far cry from the previous 'loud uproar' (15). It is curious to see the Poet exercising 'diffidence and modesty' in addressing his friend Coleridge in the present – in 'I may add' (74), 'Un-apprehensive of reproof' (75), 'perhaps too much' (77). This subtly relates the boy to the man. It also strengthens the final notion that 'solitude' was a 'power' (78).

Lines 79–98

The sophistication of 'delicate viands' (79) was unknown to them. The 'Sabines' (82) were a very early Italian tribe respected by the ancient Romans for their simplicity of morals and manners, so much so that the writer Horace possessed a 'Sabine' farm to which he retreated from the capital in order to live the simple life. We must be aware, however, not only of the meaning of 'Sabine' (82), but of the tone which Wordsworth intends. Used of small boys, it is over-heroic and high-flown, a solemn word indeed in this context. The disparity is intended so as to make us feel a comic descent from 'Sabine' to its opposite, self-indulgence, and (looking ahead) to luxurious teas of 'strawberries and mellow cream' (167). Phrases like 'vigorous hunger' (81) and 'frugal, Sabine fare' (82) may seem to celebrate a primitive, rural simplicity which gave health and strength, but Wordsworth is humorously aware that this is the man's view rather than the boys'. 'More than we wished we knew the blessing then/Of vigorous hunger' (80–1). To the boys, that is, the 'blessing' was distinctly doubtful. In fact they loved eating! Wordsworth uses a mock-heroic tone to make gentle fun of the ardent seriousness of the boys in their pursuit of food. The phrase 'pennyless poverty' (85) is mock tragic. 'To gratify the palate with repasts' (89) is mock-sophisticated. It conveys the boys' mood when, with more pocket-money, they could afford 'repasts/More costly' (89–90). A ringing tone of self-importance can be detected, too, in 'weekly stipend' (83), meaning simply 'pocket-money'. Even the dame is elevated to the heroic status of 'That ancient woman' (91) in the boys' small world. Their 'rustic dinners' (94) took place in paradisial settings (94–7). However adventurous were the 'inroads into distant vales' (92), and intense the excitement of 'Excursions far away among the hills' (93), all these experiences were circled round with a secure mood of joy: 'the sun,/Unfelt, shone sweetly round us in our joy' (97–8). 'Cool' (94), 'in the woods' (95), 'shady fountain' (96), 'soft airs' (96), 'the sun,/Unfelt' (97–8) are all images of protectiveness.

Lines 99–121

With the phrase 'Nor is my aim neglected' (99) Wordsworth reminds the reader that a high aim is paradoxically served by continuing his accounts of apparently unimportant incidents in the lives of these obscure children. 'To feel the motion of the galloping steed' (103) was now the boys' 'anxious' (102) wish. Exhilaration, delight in the physical sensation of movement, reminds us of 'Proud and exulting, like an untired horse' (I: 459). Horses, for Wordsworth, mean the pride and exultation of physical delight. Seeking this delight involved deceiving the inn-keeper, 'Sly subterfuge' (106), since the journey planned 'was too distant far/For any cautious man' (107–8). After these acts of slyness and incaution, the destination was, in contrast, 'A holy scene' (114), St Mary's Abbey ruins. The valley acted as a 'safe-guard for repose and quietness' (121). It remained undisturbed even when 'wind of roughest temper' (117) passed overhead, so that the atmosphere of the valley seemed magically unaffected by the weather. It was almost like another island, in this respect, cut off from the surrounding disturbance. The unnecessary repetition of 'Both' (119) seems to double the effect of 'silent' and 'motionless'. Repose (121) after physical exertion repeats the pattern of resting 'in the shade' (68) after rowing. The islands, like the Vale of Nightshade, had that quality of protected seclusion which was more satisfying than the games themselves.

There is the same sweet sense of the past here, but amplified, as in the third island, with its 'hermit's history' (65). The 'mouldered cave' (64) becomes the 'mouldering pile' (112) of the abbey. Note how 'mouldering pile' precedes 'living trees' (113); the contrast subtly modulates into a similarity. The verb 'mouldering' des-cribes a process as natural as 'living'. Moreover, the old dame's stone (45), the old stone table (64) and the stone abbot (half a stone, half an abbot (125)), all have the same quality of venerable age.

Lines 122–44

The sense of the past mingles with the sense of time stood still. The singing of the 'invisible bird' (132) was so sweet 'that there I could have made/My dwelling-place, and lived for ever there/To hear such music' (133–5). This takes us back to the first island, 'musical with birds/That sang for ever' (59–60); and further back to the river's 'ceaseless music' in Book I (279).

'With whip and spur' (123) strikes a harsh note, in noticeable contrast to 'sang so sweetly' (126). There is the simultaneous presence of 'giddy motion' (49) and 'calmer pleasures' (51), and the Poet definitely emphasises the disparities of mood. The horse race by the holy 'chauntry' (123) was 'uncouth' (124). The sheer speed of 'we by the chauntry flew' (123) contrasts with the statuesque stillness of the 'cross-legged knight,/And the stone abbot' (124–5). The diminutive solitude of 'that single wren' (125) points up the burly companionship of the horse-race.

Contradictions are also emphasised in the boy's actual feelings which were more complex and mixed than before. There was something about St Mary's Abbey, after all, which contrasts with the shelter and security emphasised in the previous paragraphs. Words like 'sobbings' (129), 'respirations' (130) and 'shuddering' (131) are disturbing. These sounds are as sinister as those 'Low breathings coming after me' of Book I (330). The place had an awesome remoteness both in terms of its antiquity and also its physical distance, for the boys, from home; it was a 'comfortless' (128) place. What it intimated about life and time, though not really understood by the boys, was half manifested to them. Hence, there was a somewhat hurried anxiety to get away from it – 'We scampered homeward' (138), rather like frightened mice. And so these scary feelings contrasted with the opposite momentary impulse to live 'for ever there/To hear such music' (134–5). There was, altogether, a mingling of delight and fear; 'beauty' and 'fear' (see I: 306) cannot be disentangled here in the boy's quite natural mixture of feelings.

The whole paragraph is made up of three sentences, the first of which is fourteen lines long and curiously dislocated. Paraphrased its sense would be something like – 'we left the wren which (though the earth was without comfort, and the ivy on the roofless walls, touched by breezes, sobbings and respirations dripped large drops) still sang sweetly to itself.' As it stands, however, we are allowed to lose ourselves among the wandering sub-clauses as the young Wordsworth lost *himself* in reverie. 'Through the walls we flew' (135) makes a rude intrusion as time suddenly breaks into the sense of timelessness.

Such holiday 'wantonness of heart' (137) still had the power to dispel both fear and beauty. It was an overwhelming youthful energy expressed in the furious rhythm, noise and physical enjoyment of the line, 'We beat with thundering hoofs the level sand' (144). That the 'still spirit of the evening air' (139) could yet be felt amidst all that noise and movement, emphasises its haunting power. Its 'intervenient' quality (see 206) is suggested too by the sudden way in which the Poet, in a present impulse of joy, directly addresses 'that still spirit' (139) as he writes. He seems to be interrupted himself by its presence.

Lines 145–202

'Above the crescent of a pleasant bay' (146) suggests an open prospect contrasting with the 'Vale/Of Nightshade' (110–11), whose actual name implied romantic gloom. From mouldering abbey ruins, we turn to a bright and splendid inn. Unlike St Mary's Abbey and its venerable stones, however, it is untrue to its ancient past. So the contrast is not just between decay and newness, because the brash appearance of the inn actually suggests a kind of moral decay.

Attention focuses first upon the building itself, with criticism reminding us of the 'assembly-room that perked and flared' (39). The inn was 'a splendid place' (149), not 'homely-featured' (147). As such, it did not belong or relate to the implied family of cottages, 'no . . ./Brother of the surrounding cottages' (147–8). Inside and out it was colourful ('liveries'; 'blood-red wine') and showy, with its socially superior 'chaises' (150) and 'Decanters' (151). Wordsworth draws a familiar contrast with a simple past, when 'In ancient times' (152), the inn was a 'hut' (154). 'Proud of its one bright fire and sycamore shade' (155) implies a pride that was not pride, but modest self-respect. The sparkling colours of the new sign – 'large golden characters/On the blue-frosted signboard' (157–8) – strike a note of sham improvement and gaudy sophistication. They had 'usurped' (158) the familiar old lion's place, much as the assembly-room had earlier elbowed out the old stone (40). The Poet emphasises the disrespect behind the modernisation, 'contempt/And mockery of the rustic painter's hand' (159–60).

His affections, however, have some of their roots here and so 'to this hour the spot to me is dear' (161). The location of the children's play (now bowling, more sedate than the boisterous activities of before) was a garden, a schoolboy paradise. The boy was both sensitive to the 'gleams' (165) of beauty from the lake and absorbed too in his tea of 'strawberries and mellow cream' (167) – a further example of how, in the elevated language of a previous passage, they would 'gratify the palate with repasts' (89). The initial sentiments about the inn itself are obviously the man's rather than the boy's. As yet, the boy was clearly unaware of time and change, but as readers we see evidence of them in the shape of the modernised inn, as the boy plays in the protected seclusion of the garden.

The shouts which 'Made all the mountains ring' (170) subside quietly into 'the fall/Of night' (170–1) and 'rowed off gently' (175). Again, as in the St Mary's Abbey passage, a solitary music-maker emphasised the predominant quiet, and helped to create a mood of intent, receptive listening. In this mood, the landscape seemed to enter into his heart (180). An almost physical inter-nalisation is suggested in 'weight of pleasure' (178) and 'sank down/Into my heart' (179–80). There is an implicit parallel between the sky sinking into the lake, as in a reflection, and the whole scene sinking into his heart (see V: 409–13).

'Thus' (beyond the narrow scope of the games, rowing or riding) he writes . . . 'were my sympathies enlarged' (181). His 'heart' (180), possessed by the landscape, correspondingly grew in its capacity to love. Growth of love is now the theme. 'Grew dear to me' (183) leads on to the gentle progression from 'I began/To love the sun' (183–4) to 'a boy I loved the sun' (184). Simplicity and gentleness are the keynotes. The boy thought of sunrise and sunset (usually sublime moments) in terms of intimacy and physical touch – 'lay/His beauty on the morning hills' (188–9) and 'had seen/The western mountain touch his setting orb' (189–90). The moon too, proverbially remote, was felt to be actually present in the valley. It 'hung/Midway between the hills' (198–9).

Now this strange closeness of the sun and moon, so vividly felt, fitted in with the boy's sense that his world was complete. He experienced no sense of a missing element in life which was unattainable, no wistful yearning or dissatisfaction; he felt the sublime was present in the ordinary world. And so we are reading about a condition of being in the boy which was at the opposite pole from that adult incompleteness summed up in Blake's little engraving entitled 'I WANT! I WANT!' in which a long ladder extends from earth to moon. In contrast, the boy had no need to yearn, since the moon was present in his valley.

An intimate affinity existed between the celestial and the humble. The moon belonged to the valley (200); more specifically, it 'appertained by a peculiar right' (201) to what was utterly humble and insignificant, the 'grey huts' (202) of the inhabitants. It was now on a level of equality with them. The quite natural way in which it is brought into the local community is reminiscent of Samuel Palmer's Shoreham paintings, e.g. 'Harvest Moon,' (1831–2). This is a similar representation of such a visionary landscape, the moon hanging low in the sky, quite tangible in its closeness to the humble lives of the valley dwellers.

The boy's mood was 'thoughtless' (191). Perhaps the ephemeral nature of the child's vision is suggested in the speed with which the sun rises and sets in the space of two lines (189–90). On the other hand, this cyclical movement also conveys a repetitive and static sense of time. The simplest functions, life's basic elements, were pleasures in themselves (the flowing of blood, breathing (192–3)). This spontaneity of feeling contrasts with our own more indirect mode of experience (185–7). We love the sun not simply because, as the boy, we feel its beauty (189), but because we are rationally aware of it 'as a pledge/And surety of our earthly life' (185–6). This awareness makes us (as adults) 'feel we are alive' (187). It is sadly ironic that, unlike the child, we need a rational motivation to give us the confidence to feel something. In a final nostalgic endearment, 'my darling vale' (202), the Poet reminds us how strong remains his attachment to this locality as the source of his affections.

BOOK II

Lines 203–37

So the 'incidental charms' (203) – games – which had 'attached/My heart to rural objects' (203–4) lost importance as Nature, now paramount in his affections, was 'sought/For her own sake' (207–8). It is this announcement of a decisive turning-point in his imaginative development which suddenly diverts him into a consideration of such over-precise classifications.

We focus upon the Poet's own method of self-analysis. Wordsworth pulls himself up short ('But who shall parcel out/His intellect . . .?' (208–9)) and checks the careful division of his life into stages. He dislikes having to 'parcel out' (208) or 'Split' (210) – reduce to parts – according to a system ('geometric rules' (209)) which is artificially imposed. Personal development is more of a growth (the seed metaphor (212)) or a continuous flow (the river metaphor (214)). This last analogy best exposes the sheer absurdity of psychological analysis. How can you isolate a 'portion' (214) of flowing water or trace its precise source? Coleridge, Wordsworth modestly affirms, is more deeply read in his own thoughts (216). He sees science (or analysis) for what it is, a substitute ('succedaneum' (219)), a help or tool ('a prop/To our infirmity' (219–20)). He is not enslaved by 'that false secondary power' (221). Imagination, of course, is the primary power. He rightly sees science as man's creation and not absolute truth. Its 'distinctions' (222) and 'puny boundaries' (223) are not realities, but inventions (224). Coleridge, seeing them as superficial ('outward shows' (225)) is able to penetrate through to the profounder unity (226) which scientific analysis fragments. In other words, Coleridge possesses an active and unifying imagination. Doubting the value (227) of dividing the mind into compartments and stages, Wordsworth considers how false it is to 'Run through the history and birth of each/As of a single independent thing' (230–1). The theme of this Book is, after all, the 'one life' (430), unity, and the Poet realises that his adult impulse to categorise goes against his youthful sense. He also feels that it is contrary to the vision of his friend, Coleridge.

Just as the stages of his life overlap and inter-connect in complex

unity, so too do their causes or beginnings. His modest hesitations
('less aptly skilled' (227); 'Hard task' (232)) therefore express, not
his own inadequacy, but that of analysis itself. Each 'soul' (232) is
a unity, and all its parts ('general habits and desires' (233); 'each
most obvious and particular thought' (234)) are inter-linked. The
scientific search for causes (230) ignores the one great fact which
imagination (or deepest reason (236)) sees clearly – that no single
cause can ever be isolated in the complex process of mental
growth. Each thought (and the stress falls equally on each word)
'Hath no beginning' (237).

Lines 237–80

'Hath no beginning' (237) seems to pre-empt any further consideration of the origins of mind and personality, but the second
half of the line boldly brings in their beginning, 'the infant babe'
(237). The topic is re-opened at source, but in the imaginative
spirit of 'best conjectures' (238), not scientific analysis. 'Blessed
the infant babe' (237) and 'blest the babe' (239) seem at first to be in
a tone of affection pure and simple. This is enforced by the
physical warmth, touch and protectiveness of 'Nursed in his
mother's arms' (240) and 'sleeps/Upon his mother's breast'
(240–1). Suddenly, however, the babe seems less diminutive and
'blessed' takes on a spiritual meaning. The babe is a 'soul' (241)
who, quite imperiously, 'Claims manifest kindred with an earthly
soul' (242). It seems alien, commanding and celestial. 'Hath no
beginning' takes on a new sense. The babe's 'beginning' is not
'earthly', with its mother, but, by implication, celestial, with
God. The proud, sonorous tone of line 242 swiftly changes into
the more human and hungry excitement of 'Doth gather passion
from his mother's eye' (243). This soul is not isolated and spiritual
because it delights to feed upon sensation (the mother's touch) and
feeling, 'passion'. We have a sense of freshness and exhilaration in
the phrase 'Like an awakening breeze' (245), which echoes the
inspirational metaphor of the poem's own 'beginning'.
  The babe's inspiration is its mother. From the interchange with

her, the child's mind acquires its unique unifying power, becoming 'eager to combine/In one appearance all the elements/ And parts of the same object, else detached/And loth to coalesce' (247–50). These lines refer to the baby's elementary but vital ability to make visual shapes out of the chaotic blur of light which it first sees. The unifying power of imagination starts with this elementary leap in perception, inspired by the mother (257–8). In this way, love itself is the essential prime impulse enabling the senses (e.g. sight) to create coherent shapes out of chaos. The child's mind (250–4) acquires the ability to order and unify, and here the word 'discipline' (251) as applied to love, is important. It undermines any preconceptions about the ineffective 'softness' of motherly love. As a 'discipline', her love imparts the very ability to see. Love and perception are bound together.

What is more, the pattern of a loving relationship (an inter-change of giving and taking) becomes the actual pattern of all real imaginative experience. 'From Nature largely he receives, nor so/Is satisfied, but largely gives again' (267–8). This relationship with Nature, growing out of that with the mother, comes to have the force of both natural law ('gravitation' (263)) and loving family loyalty ('filial bond' (263)). The first suggests an external force driving him; the second phrase, a voluntary response. It is an experience both passive and active. 'No outcast he' (261) and 'inmate of this *active* universe' (266) also stress a powerful sense of belonging. All that has been said hitherto in Book II about belong-ing or not belonging (e.g. the moon, the inn) leads up to this crucial passage. Belonging has been a preoccupation of the Book so far, and this passage demonstrates the primary source of that pattern of relationship.

'Even as an agent of the one great mind' (272) recalls the child's origin and as God's messenger, his mind possesses an element of God's creative power (273). This power is a continuing process, however, not a single one-way act. The phrase 'creator and receiver' (273) reminds us that *relationship* is the vital imaginative pattern. It is a fresh, child-like 'Poetic spirit' (276) which adult 'controul' (277) sometimes suppresses. Only 'in some' (278) does

[45]

it survive. We sense Wordsworth's apprehension about time's corrosive effects.

Lines 280–303

Physical 'touch' (282) was the first way in which an interchange of feelings took place. Expressions such as 'intercourse' (282) and 'mute dialogues' (283) convey that Wordsworth thinks of touch here as an expressive, pre-verbal language. This subtle ability to communicate and respond to feeling – 'the infant sensibility' (285) in fact – was 'Augmented and sustained' (287) by Nature. All the experiences described prior to the babe passage, were 'the means' (284) by which he had been sustained until this teenage time. The word 'means' recalls Book I (362), 'Thanks likewise for the means!' As there, it implies a hidden intention and an ultimate end or purpose.

The phrase 'a path/More difficult before me' (287–8) refers again to the actual making of the poem and recalls the journey metaphor of lines 1–3. Here the poem's progress has become a difficult mountain climb (289–90). The 'chamois' (290), an alpine deer expert at keeping a footing on precipitous rocks, suggests this. The 'eagle's wing' (290) expresses aspiration; the implied mountain wilderness figures the difficult, exploratory nature of the topic. 'We' (289) are reader and writer in this companionship of ascent and aspiration (see III: 168–9 for a similar ascent of the poem in exploration of its topic).

'From unknown causes' (292) and 'nor knowing why' (293) suggest mystery, but not to be regretted. These phrases need to be linked with Wordsworth's whole argument (208–37) against analysis. The 'trouble' (291) was the sudden independence and turmoil of adolescence. The 'props' (294) removed were the games which had supported his love of Nature. This is the final stage in the part played by them in his life. Originally, games dominated, though Nature occasionally intervened. Secondly, Nature became a necessary background to the games, their enjoyment depending upon its presence (see 48–78). Now, thirdly, Nature was sought for its own sake. As 'incidental charms' (203), the games had weakened in influence; now, they were removed altogether. The momentary sensation of troubled isolation soon passed into one of increased relationship, heightened 'communion' (300) with Nature.

This communion was first experienced as a new alertness in the sense of sight, an ability to notice 'minuter properties/Of objects' (301–2) with increased sensitivity. This new sharpness depended upon love. Just as the 'mother's heart' (283) fed the child's ability to see, so now love ('our hearts', 300) was the prerequisite for finer perception. This is stressed. We notice the minuter properties of 'objects which already are beloved,/And of those only' (302–3). Notice the insistence of the last four words. We can only see the unique qualities of what we *already* love. Thus sight actually depends upon love.

Lines 303–41

The child now learns in a mood of increasing happiness because 'every hour brings palpable access/Of knowledge' (305–6). This word 'knowledge', repeated in line 306 as if to focus our attention upon it, was not book-knowledge, but as the end-word in the line emphasises, 'delight' (306). It was a matter of feeling rather than reason and came from Nature and not school, making an odd irony of the Book's title, 'School-time'. This knowledge of the natural world was learnt through the senses of sight (307–21) and hearing (323–9). These were given sharp alertness by love, whose invigorating capacity is expressed in the phrase 'watchful power' (310).

Love, in effect, taught the eye to see. The season's 'transitory qualities' (309), which might otherwise pass by unnoticed, were actively brought to his notice (308). An eye uninspired by love would have 'neglected' (311) to see them, even if it had actually looked at them. The point is that we do not always see what we are looking at. In this child's case, however, a 'register/Of permanent relations' (311–12) was established. The word 'register' here implies noticing (as in the verb 'to register'), as well as record, so that this last phrase means 'a lasting recognition of these established affections'. Lines 318–19 refer again to the child's ability to see with precise discrimination and so increase his responsiveness. Love (310) inspired the development of a sharp visual awareness.

We now pass from 'silent inobtrusive sympathies' (316) to the more disturbing 'power in sound' (324), from 'gentle agitations of the mind' (317) to 'Sublimer joy' (321). This joy was nevertheless 'from the same source' (320) – that is, from the 'watchful power of love' (310). 'To breathe an elevated mood' (325) suggests the inspirational excitement of Book I (41–5), a heightened communion. The primitive, pre-verbal language of elemental sound, 'The ghostly language' (328) in which 'the ancient earth' (328) communicated, follows quite naturally from the primitive (equally non-verbal) language of touch (282–3), in which his mother communicated. Touch, sight and hearing constitute a language of the senses through which the child learns. The drinking image (330) gives the intensity of physical appetite to the purely visionary. Even such elevated moods were rooted in the world of sense.

Nevertheless, they possessed a tenuous quality, as 'shadowy' (332) and 'fleeting' (331) suggest. Memory of them is uncertain – 'Remembering' (335), but also 'Remembering not' (336). The mind seems active in this refining of the essential feeling ('how she felt' (335)) from otherwise forgotten experiences. The soul continued to grow and aspire (338–9), feeding upon these glimpses of 'possible sublimity' (337). Just as it had 'no beginning' (237), it likewise has no end, and 'still [has] something to pursue' (340–1). It is subject to no limits, the implication being that it is eternal. Lines 336–41 describe a dimly apprehended sense of this (337), and the endlessly mounting ascent (337–41) towards an unattainable goal.

Lines 341–71

'And not alone' (341) tugs against 'I would walk alone' (321) and 'I was left alone' earlier (292), reminding us that this apparent new isolation involved hidden relationships with Nature. The 'universal power' (343) communicated with him through the 'latent qualities/And essences of things' (344–5). In a complementary direction, Wordsworth the boy communicated with the 'universal power'; the 'superadded soul' (347) within him actually 'strengthened' (347) it. 'And not alone' is further supported by the companionship of his 'friend/Then passionately loved' (352–3). Imaginative affinity is important here as later with his sister, Dorothy, and Coleridge. We may recall how later the 'green pastoral landscape' of Tintern Abbey was to be made 'More dear' because he saw it with his much-loved sister. Notice how here, too, being with his friend made the pleasant wandering round the lake 'more dear' (351), strengthening his feeling for the landscape. This was an instance of how companionship could be 'made sweet as solitude/By silent inobtrusive sympathies' (315–16). But time divides; 'for many years/Have since flowed in between us' (355–6). Wordsworth hopes (in similar mood to line 43) for a momentary return of their friendship; 'With heart how full/Will he peruse these lines' (353–4). Times of solitude when not with his friend ('among the hills I sate/Alone' (361–2)) were yet moments of intense communion – 'solitude/More active even than "best society" ' (313–14). There was an answering 'utter solitude' (364) in the vale itself. The communion was so complete that inside and outside seemed to coalesce. The landscape appeared to be 'A prospect in my mind' (371). This dream-like transport, when the scene seemed internalised, echoes the earlier experience (179–80) when the sky 'sank down/Into my heart, and held me like a dream'. The religious tone occurs again – 'a holy calm/Did overspread my soul' (367–8). An element of the celestial, as opposed to the 'bodily' (369) or earthly enters into the experience. 'How shall I trace the history, where seek/The origin of what I then have felt?' (365–6). The Poet reiterates the argument of lines 208–37 against rational analysis and the enquiring after causes. Unearthly experiences can hardly be explained in such a way.

Lines 371–95

Lines 371–5 recall the phrase 'delightful round' in Book I (504), and in this Book the phrase 'round of tumult' (9) and 'the year span round' (48). The cyclical movement is even more insistent now, with 'spring and autumn' (372), 'winter snows' and 'summer shade' (372–3), 'day and night' (373), 'The evening and the morning' (374), 'dreams' and 'waking thoughts' (374–5). Time's gentle motion served only to 'nurse' (375) him, in his loving companionship with Nature (376–7). He insists that, although he was nearing his seventeenth year (405) he still retained the 'creative sensibility' (379: see also 285) of earliest childhood. Time had not subdued it (380–1), but nursed it.

This creative sensibility was 'plastic' (formative) and a 'power' (381). Certain words and phrases emphasise the element of power – 'Rebellious' (383), 'at war' (384), 'Subservient' (386), 'obeyed/A like dominion' (391–2). This power, when in its rebellious and devious mood (383), might be compared to the wayward 'creative breeze' of Book I (43–8). When 'Subservient' (386), on the other hand, to Nature (386), communion or two-way relationship was possible. 'Subservient' recalls that love (251) is ideally a discipline and that relationship, rather than isolation (384), is the true imaginative pattern. Compare lines 261–8.

The 'auxiliar light' (387) shining from his mind is a powerful metaphor for creative imagination. It recalls that God's first creative act was light. 'And God said, Let there be light, and there was light' (Genesis I: 3). The metaphor implies that the imagination is a 'godlike power' (IV: 156). Its origin is, in a sense, celestial (see line 272). It seems to re-create the world. The notion of the 'auxiliar light' giving an extra 'splendor' (389) to the sun, the source of light itself, is striking. Different elements of the natural world, though retaining their own innate beauty (391), acquired an additional brilliance. Conversely, the darkness of the 'midnight storm' (392) was intensified.

From a stress on companionship ('I walked with Nature' (377)), we have passed to an emphasis on power. Lines 394–5, however, remind us that even this creative power was a means to a more intense communion. 'Hence my obeisance, my devotion hence,/ And hence my transport.' In this spiritual progression from humility to exhilaration, the devoted obedience to Nature cannot be separated from his creative power over it. There is a pattern of receptivity and control – in other words, a relationship, but here moving beyond that to a purer communion, a total immersion of his feelings (417–18) in Nature's 'overflowing soul' (416).

Lines 395–434

The emotional tone of this paragraph ascends from disarming self-depreciation ('Nor should this, perchance,/Pass unrecorded' (395–6)) to a transcendence of self in which confidence or modesty are irrelevant. The note of hesitancy suggests that the major experience of this section needs no argument or persuasive introduction. The author draws back to allow the Book's climax (420–8) to speak for itself.

There is a gradual preparation of the ground, recalling passages already familiar. The unifying 'Creative agency' (401) was more pleasing than 'analytic industry' (398), that fragmenting power already attacked in lines 208–37. The 'observation of affinities/In objects where no brotherhood exists/To common minds' (403–5) was the complementary, cementing tendency to that awareness earlier of 'manifold distinctions, difference/Perceived in things where to the common eye/No difference is' (318–20).

Lines 405–13 enumerate a number of possible explanations of the experience about to be described. They by no means exclude each other and undermine the destructive process of analysis by avoiding any single explanation or cause of his new mood. The syntax itself ('whether' (406); 'or' (407); 'or' (411)) opens up possibilities and sets no rational limits. The alternative put forward is particularly important. 'To unorganic natures I transferred/My own enjoyments' (410–11) describes a process of psychological projection of his feelings on to what he saw in the landscape. Alternatively, 'I conversed/With things that really are' (412–13) suggests the real, objective existence of the new spirit.

He cannot decide, even looking back, whether what he saw was actually external or only in his mind. His analytical diffidence deliberately blurs the line between subjective experience and objective reality, leading on to the 'one life' (430) which breaks down boundaries between the individual self and the outside world.

After this abstract philosophising, we encounter a physical metaphor. 'I at this time/Saw blessings spread around me like a sea' (413–14). This liquidity continues both in terms of imagery and the rhythmic flow of 420–8. 'Nature and her overflowing soul' (416) carries forward the water imagery introduced by 'sea' and signifies a fullness of spiritual grace. Compare Psalm 23: 'my cup runneth over'. Finally, 'my thoughts/Were steeped in feeling' (417–18) proclaims the full immersion of baptism. The emotional intensity continues to 'bliss ineffable' (419) and the sustained lyricism of 420–8.

These lines stand out from the thoughtful abstraction and expansive syntax of the surrounding lines in their lyrical simplicity of rhythm and language. Every aspect of style and expression helps to create a sense of the unifying 'one life'. Monosyllables make line 425 a perfect iambic pentameter with a regular rhythm and flow. Apparent contrast in meaning, in line 421, suddenly dissolves into unity; the antithesis is false because 'seemeth still' *means* 'moves'. The second half of the line merely repeats the first half, rather than apparently setting up an opposition.

The disparate energies of innumerable animals, birds, insects, fishes (and children) merge into a single energy expressed in the rhythm and active verbs (425–6). Notice how the creatures are unnamed and unspecified (individualising nouns are avoided) except in terms of their energies (the verbs) which all unite into a single rhythm, the 'one life' (430). The happy noise of 'shouts' and 'sings' takes us back to the 'loud uproar' (15) of the children's play. The universal 'joy' (430) obviously moved in them, too.

There was a melting of his own separateness into a sense of the great whole at this time. He felt lifted up into some higher 'bliss' (419), and was 'lost beyond the reach of thought/And human knowledge' (422–3). The world of the senses was left behind because mere sight, 'the human eye' (423), and hearing, 'the fleshly ear' (432), were inadequate to a complete perception of this 'one life'. Only the 'heart' (424), source of all perception as argued earlier (300), can fully experience it. The heart is therefore more subtly responsive than either the senses or thought.

The lyrical rhythm and energy appropriately culminate in a musical metaphor. 'One song they sang' (431). Like Keats's 'ditties of no tone' ('Ode on a Grecian Urn') it was 'audible-/Most audible' (431–2) to the spirit or the heart.

Lines 435–66

This paragraph, like the previous one, starts on a note of uncertainty and ascends again to joy (465). This joy is not the enveloping one (430) of youth, but the more abstract 'never-failing principle' (465) of maturity. What remains of the youth's visionary joy, however supportive (464–5), is an adult 'faith' (459) and not a feeling of transport (429). Something of the doubt suggested in line 435 is endemic to adulthood as the phrase 'this uneasy heart of ours' (464) admits.

Maintaining the vision is also difficult in the Poet's historical circumstances. Due to the failure of the French Revolution ('This melancholy waste of hopes o'erthrown' (449)), Wordsworth finds himself in a world of ideals in collapse, and peopled by those hostile to everything visionary (455–6). We need to realise here that his expectations of the Revolution were that human nature would be reborn (see Book VI: 354). There would, he hoped, be a return to a sinless state of happiness for mankind, 'a paradise of ages' (see Book X: 321). Now this has failed, he turns to an alternative paradise, the happy state of childhood, in which, as an adult, he has found unfailing 'support' (460).

Though the eroding cynicism with which the mature Poet feels himself surrounded might encourage self-doubt (435), his reaction is defiance. First, even the mere mention of error will enforce the truth of his best insights to those who recognise the echo of Shakespeare's Sonnet 116, 'If this be error and upon me

proved,/I never writ nor man ever loved.' Secondly, the two
negative 'if' clauses (435 and 439) which intrude an initial doubt
are triumphantly cancelled out in a mountaing sentence (443–62)
of five positive 'if' clauses. With its emphasis on the phrase 'more
than Roman confidence' (459), the sentence itself is self-con-
sciously 'Roman' in its courageous and declamatory rhetoric. It
perhaps owes its inspiration to such devices of classical, formal
rhetoric as 'climax' (Greek for 'ladder', signifying a sentence
which mounts in rungs) and 'anaphora' (repetition). We need to
realise here how French Republican idealists would think of themselves as 'Roman' in their love of liberty. 'Roman' (like 'Sabine'
(82)) was synonymous with 'upright' and 'austere'. The moral
simplicity celebrated in his peroration, however, is 'more than
Roman' (459); the Poet resorts to yet a purer ideal ('Nature' (446,
462)), inspiring even greater confidence. So we mount yet further
(the rhetorical language of Republican idealism serves a greater
end) to the height of 'Ye mountains!' (462) and the phrase 'lofty
speculations' (463). Notice, therefore, that proclamation of the
visionary is now an act of defiant rhetoric, not an easy lyrical song
(420–8).

Lines 466–84

Lines 466–79 return to a friendly, intimate tone. Coleridge's
friendship consoles him in a cynical world. We end on the note of
companionship with which the Book began (478), and with a
sense of a destination reached (468–9).

Lines 479–84 admire that paradox of solitude in relationship
which Coleridge's life means to Wordsworth. His reclusiveness
(482) will yet be 'a blessing to mankind' (484).

Pattern of thought

Unity is the 'argument' of this Book in a variety of ways. First,
there is an insistent note of companionship and togetherness. The

social harmony between old and young (1–47) leads on to the companionable pursuits of rowing races (48–78), picnicking (79–98) and horse-riding (99–144). There is a paradise atmosphere, secluded islands, magically peaceful spots. There is a mood of total satisfaction and composure, so that rivalry is unnecessary. And there is a static quality, as if time were arrested. The boy is not immersed in pure sensation and fantasy, as he was in Book I. He had an emotional response to the natural world, especially to his home valley. The harmony between the celestial and the humble enhances the sense of protected enclosure. Physical energy and boisterousness gave way to a more spiritual calm. The second half of the Book contrasts in style with the first in its more densely philosophical and speculative language. This is introduced, however, by a paragraph which, on an intellectual level, is concerned with the Book's main topic, unity (203–37). The poet is concerned to check the tendency to fragmenting analysis in his own writing. Following on from this, he traces the origins of that opposite, unifying power in the mind. These are to be found in the baby's first responses to the world. Childhood is demonstrably linked to adulthood in a sustained piece of synthesis (237–341). In these lines, Wordsworth's sentences take on a complexity which suggests intellectual grappling. Yet their topic is the growth of the senses and feeling. We are invited to consider the processes of the heart with our heads. Love is seen as an active power in a universe of powers and forces. These powers interpenetrate in the physical, emotional, and perceptual worlds.

Imaginative companionship (with a childhood friend (341–53)) is then taken up and, finally, this sociable reaction to the scene gives way to a fuller and more personal communion. This reaches its intensest moment when, aged seventeen, he had a vision of the unity of all natural life. The penultimate paragraph (435–66) records how the mature poet still draws sustenance from 'Nature' (462), though we may feel that the ecstasy of the youthful joy has paled into a memory. The final address to Coleridge, more personal than any other concluding address, fittingly intensifies the theme of companionship.

BOOK III

Lines 1–15

Wordsworth approached Cambridge on an inauspicious morning. The weather was dreary and the landscape, unlike the one he was used to, significantly flat. Something of a subdued tone will characterise his attitude to Cambridge throughout the Book and these first impressions give the reader an indication of what to expect. Both the town itself and his life there are consistently described throughout as essentially unreal and the 'pinnacles' (5) rising above the groves are the first hint of the almost fairy-tale nature of what he saw.

There quickly followed another unreal 'vision' – a student who 'passed' (8) leaving him gaping. The famous university town appeared to draw him into itself as though into a whirlpool ('eddy' (11)). There is something sinister about this and the whirlpool image is appropriate to the whirl of disconnected and bewildering impressions which confused him there. The inn's name, 'Hoop', another circle image, suggests perhaps something one had to go through to enter, or maybe a catch or trap.

Lines 16–43

He was excited and full of expectation (16), but also distracted, which was uncharacteristic of him. This was a 'world/Of welcome faces' (19–20), a confusing and superficial place though not without attraction. Here acquaintance passed for friendship (17–18), the first of many suggestions that depth of relationships did not play much part in Cambridge life. Exclamatory phrases, such as 'Fresh day/Of pride and pleasure' (22–3) draw our attention to another aspect of the Book, the ironic and gently self-mocking. Phrases like 'pride and pleasure', 'loose and careless' (23, 27) suggest sinfulness, indulgence, loss of direction, and lack of diligence, and occur throughout the description of his new independence. This was no quiet independence of the heart but rather self-importance and vanity. He found no real people in Cambridge, only types adopting roles or striking attitudes. There are, therefore, many images of clothes and fashion. One of his first 'sights' was a 'gown and tasselled cap' (7). His former schoolfriends were 'hung round/With honour and importance' (18–19), and 'tutors' and 'tailors' (26) are mentioned in the same breath.

The clothing imagery is extended in this paragraph. He roamed through the 'motley spectacle' (29) (motley = fool's dress) with its suggestion of the theatrical coming close to the clownish and ludicrous. He was 'attired' (35) in 'splendid clothes' (36), 'hose of silk' (36) and now in his maturity he facetiously dismisses his 'lordly dressing-gown' (38) which was a particularly memorable part of his 'gentleman's array' (43). Again, he remarks that the whole experience was a 'dream' (28), a fairy-tale. The transformation from 'northern villager' to rich gentleman 'As if by word/Of magic or some fairy's power' (33–4) is indeed like the Cinderella story, but the underlying sense is that such transformations are not really possible and money, clothes, 'invitations, suppers, wine' (41), and so on, do not transform one overnight. 'Smooth housekeeping within, and all without/Liberal' (42–3) suggests that he was in danger of coming to believe that life was really like that.

Lines 44–59

The trumpeting tone of the first line ('The Evangelist St John my patron was') collapses instantly into the skulking 'Three gloomy courts are his' (45). There is a hint that the Saint as Evangelist or preacher of truth has long been abandoned by the college which bears his name. The sense of the clear call of the Gospel going out to the four corners of the earth is contrasted here with the inward-looking courts and 'nook obscure' (46). St John's College was much more mundane and much less inspiring than the young Wordsworth would have liked.

Immediately we are among the college kitchens where we are reminded of low life and of the frenzied and laborious activity which went into producing the 'smooth housekeeping' and liberality of gentlemanly life so 'approvingly' described in the previous paragraph. There is, in addition to the seriousness of the theme here, a touch of humour when we see that after all his pretensions to grandeur Wordsworth in fact occupied an 'obscure' nook over these kitchens. From the obscurity, though, we gradually approach the illustrious figure of Newton. Although Newton was clearly everything that the young Cambridge intellectual might aspire to be, he becomes, later in the Book, an example of humility, 'Even the great Newton's own etherial self,/Seemed humbled in these precincts' (270–1). True greatness, Wordsworth seems to be saying, is in humility and not in an ostentatious display of power and glory. Newton's marble statue had a sublime silence and its presence at the end of this paragraph contrasts with the noise and distraction which precedes – the constant 'humming sound' (48) of the college kitchens, the 'shrill notes' (49) of the staff, the interminable disturbance of the 'loquacious clock' (51) which, he complains, would never let things be but marked off each division of the hour and did so twice over, and finally the 'pealing organ' (55) of Trinity Chapel. The contrast, moreover, was not just between noise and silence, but between talkativeness (the humming and loquacity) and the mysterious wordless silence of pure thought suggested by Newton's statue. The 'silent face' (59), as the climax of this noisy paragraph, contrasts subtly with every preceding sound, whether it is the proud pealing organ or the entirely mindless but talkative clock.

Lines 60–120

He now goes on to describe different types of students he knew at Cambridge. He gives a wry look back to events which had importance at the time, though less so now, 'Examinations, when the man was weighed/As in the balance' (65–6). It was not, he came to recognise, the business of Cambridge to judge the worth of a man. In Book IV we find a judicious self-examination, 'I took/The balance in my hand and weighed myself' (148–9). Because of a sense of dissatisfaction, either from his own expectations of what a Cambridge education should be, or because his family expected something of him, or because he worried about his prospects, he tended to be melancholy (72–8). He continued to think of himself as 'a chosen son' (82) who was 'not for that hour/Nor for that place' (80–1). His true function was to be both active and passive, 'to work or feel' (84), receptive to whatever was offered him, yet imaginatively strong enough to transform what he received (85–8). It is only when such interchange is possible that a man is truly free. 'I was a freeman', he writes, therefore, 'in the purest sense/Was free, and to majestic ends was strong' (89–90).

The noble purpose is important. He began his poem by dreaming about a glorious work to be undertaken (I: 123ff), an 'end' which would do justice to his poetic vocation by giving adequate expression to his intelligence. The resulting poem consistently seeks to describe the ultimate purpose of experience, 'Praise to the end' (I: 361). He was so confident in his purpose and his gifts that the mere knowledge that he possessed them was sufficient to carry him through any new situation in which he found himself – ' 'twas enough for me/To know that I was otherwise endowed' (92–3). This sense of inner depth, of a durable and maturing interior confidence to which he could resort contrasted with the surfaces of Cambridge life. There, all was 'glitter' and 'dazzle' (94–5), alluring the eyes but failing to capture the mind which 'with a rebound' (96) returned 'Into its former self' (97). It was as though Cambridge was a place on which the mind could not fix or take root. There was to be no seed-time here as there *had* been earlier, only surface attachments. Although his circumstances were now different his habits were similar. He sought apartness and solitude. 'Oft did I leave/My comrades, and the crowd' (97-8) recalls, 'Not seldom from the uproar I retired . . . leaving the tumultuous throng' in the skating episode of Book I (474-6). Like a painter standing back from his canvas to appreciate better what he is painting, Wordsworth found that distance from his habitual environment enabled him to recognise his own powers more directly (101-6). His sense of a rightness in natural things directed his intellectual enquiries. What he sought was a comparable inner logic to that which he saw in 'The common countenance of earth and heaven' (111). Like Newton, he looked for 'universal things' (110) and these were to be as crucial to an understanding of the mind as the scientific principle of gravity was, for example, to the behaviour of matter. The language of this section implies that he was on the verge of some great scientific discovery. He concentrated intensely, 'turning the mind in upon itself' (112) and, like Newton again perhaps, 'Pored, watched, expected, listened' (113). Furthermore, we feel that he was being directed in his activities as though he were in the hands of a larger power. The process was a steadily intensifying commitment to the task, one to which he was at first 'awakened' and finally 'constrained' (109). Like Samuel in the Old Testament (I Samuel 3) he was 'summoned, rouzed' (109) and initiated into a 'community with highest truth' (120). The recollection of the process excites him as he describes it and he feels obliged to check himself, 'But peace' (118).

Lines 121–67

Everything external received the transforming power of his active intelligence which gave meaning to what it animated. His mind was vital, 'not to be subdued' (123), supplying 'analogies' (122) in the moral world for the humblest things of Nature, 'Even the loose stones that cover the highway' (125). The life of Nature was linked closely, therefore, to his own life so that he had no feelings of exclusion but rather a sense that everything made up a 'great whole' (131). His susceptibilities to terror, love, and beauty (132–3) in Nature were as responsive as water, or as finely tuned as an aeolian harp to the movement of the wind (135–8). Such 'sympathies' (145) enabled him to feel privileged whether in solitude or in company, yet also, he feels, made him sometimes an odd figure to other people when his great excitement would reveal itself in 'outward gestures' and 'visible looks' (146). This behaviour got him a reputation for 'madness' (147) but the mounting rhetoric of 'if' clauses (148–51) pours scorn on the kind of 'tutored' (154) society which would label as mad the more primitive and venerable responses of 'joy' (148), 'inspiration' (150), and 'prophesy' (151). The word 'tutored' (154) reminds us of Cambridge rationalism and Wordsworth firmly suggests that only an 'undisordered sight' (155) is capable of responding as he does. 'But leaving this,/It was no madness' (155–6) summarily dismisses such criticism and is a statement of complete confidence in himself. The paragraph ends with a suggestion that perhaps, like Newton, he saw a 'perpetual logic' (165) in the myriad forms of nature, from the smallest 'stone' (161) to the 'kindred multitudes of stars' (163). This logic, notice, was perceived by his visionary 'eye' (156–60) and apprehended by his 'soul' (165). It must have been a spiritual logic, not a rational one, referring to the links of feeling which bound the universe together for him. Not only fruit and flowers but rocks and stones (124–5) had 'feelings'. There was no part of the physical world which was seen as more dead, or alive, than another. Even a 'withered leaf' (161) had life, like its parent 'tree' (161). There was no part of the physical world, moreover, which was less 'moral' or 'spiritual' than another. The life-giving 'soul' (128) appeared everywhere, even in 'loose stones' (125). The word 'loose' carries a weight of implication. The stones might seem loose, but the word 'linked' (127) binds them together in that pattern described later as a 'chain' (167). And even *they* had a 'moral life' (126). There seems to be no hierarchy of inanimate, sensuous, rational, moral, and spiritual. All these levels inter-link and overlap, so that stones *feel*; the 'eye' (160) sees a 'logic' (165); the logic is spiritual. The physical world, the 'great mass' (127), seemed to grow in a kind of spiritual soil – 'Lay bedded in a quickening soul' (128). One might say that for Wordsworth there was no distinction between the world of physics and the moral world of feelings. Compare this passage about the 'one presence' (130) with that in Book II on the 'one life' (430). We are reminded, after all, that this is a track 'not untrod before' (121). The student's awareness was less ecstatic, more thoughtful (122), consisting of complex, interlinked 'consciousnesses' (123), moral (126), spiritual (128), sensory (156), rational (165). His eye searched for 'shades of difference' (158) between various things from top to bottom on the chain of being, and the unrelenting agency of the external logic bound his 'feelings' (167) to that chain. The mounting verse pattern from humble 'withered leaf' (161) to 'stars' (163) suggests a sublime possession. These remarks recall one of Shelley's comments to Godwin in a letter of 1817 –

> I am formed, – if for anything not in common with the herd of mankind – to apprehend minute & remote distinctions of feeling whether relative to external nature, or the living beings which surround us, & to communicate the conceptions which result from considering either the moral or the material universe as a whole (I,577).[1]

Lines 168–94

He pauses at this point to reflect on all that he has been saying. From this 'eminence' (169) of his inner life the rest of the Book is a descent. The eminence is not only a high point from which he can see his own progress but a particular kind of distinction. He was no 'eminent' University scholar but was distinguished because of what he had achieved – 'Not . . . outward things/Done visibly for other minds' (174–5) but a private inner sense of 'genius, power,/

Creation, and divinity' (171–2). All this 'awful . . . might' (178)
had been established in childhood before he ever saw Cambridge.
It was essentially *untutored*, uncultivated, belonging to a much
earlier time of his life when the world was nothing but a 'wild field'
(181) where his soul was 'sown' (181). Like Milton, who claims
the Christian virtues to be more fitting subjects for an epic poem
than the traditional military ones (*Paradise Lost* IX: 25ff.),
Wordsworth, too, justifies his poem as no less 'heroic argument,/
And genuine prowess' (182–3). But, unlike Milton, he goes on to
acknowledge that much of what he has to say is 'far hidden from
the reach of words' (185). Every man has to some extent an
unreachable part of his being that belongs to him alone ('Points
have we all of us within our souls/Where all stand single' (186–7))
and because he knows this ('this I feel') Wordsworth feels he can
do no more than simply make 'Breathings' for certain powers
which are 'incommunicable' (188). The value of language itself is
again being called into question. The verse has a nice balance
between, on the one hand, his sense of the inefficacy of his attempt
and, on the other, a confidence that what he is saying will be
understood. For it is precisely beause each person *has* a sense of
'incommunicable powers' within him that he is likely to know
what Wordsworth means – 'therefore . . . I am not heartless; for
there's not a man/That lives who hath not had his god-like hours,/
And knows not what majestic sway we have/As natural beings in
the strength of Nature' (190–4).

Lines 195–236

Reflection is succeeded by a determination to press on,
'Enough . . ./We must descend' (195–6). He descends from the
'eminence' of his inner life to the 'populous plain' (195) of his
social life, introducing a piece of quiet wit, 'A traveller I am,/And
all my tale is of myself' (196–7). This tale is not, after all, going to
be a sensationalist one about adventures in exotic parts, like a
traditional traveller's tale. Our expectations are undermined in the
same way as they are in *Lyrical Ballads* when we find the

traditional narrative element of the ballad being subverted in pursuit of lyrical feeling. Wordsworth's life journey is equated with the effort of writing the poem, itself a kind of journey in which he will sometimes need the assurance of Coleridge, his understanding 'honored friend' (199) to 'Uphold' his 'fainting steps' (201). The 'populous plain' through which his life journey took him, implies a misunderstanding, disregarding, mass of men among whom he walks like Milton's Abdiel 'Unshaken, unseduced, unterrified' (*Paradise Lost* V: 899). The act of writing the poem is a similarly virtuous enterprise in which he senses he may be misunderstood, but where he also feels confident in himself 'if the pure in heart delight/To follow me' (198–9, cp. 'Blessed are the pure in heart for they shall see God' (Matt. 5: 8)).

From this pause which serves him as a girding up of loins, he launches immediately, but with spiritual confidence, into the enemy territory of 'empty noise/And superficial pastimes' (211–12). Instead of communing with his better self which was to give 'deep quiet and majestic thoughts' (210) due 'Observance' (207), he now became 'less devout' (207). Not only had he *clothed* himself in an 'outward coat' (208) as Cambridge life demanded, but he was also *adapting* to his surroundings, 'changing' his coat (209) like an animal in winter. This happened 'slowly and insensibly' (209). His nature was being changed as though he had no control over what was happening. In being so betrayed he was betraying his best self. This 'treasonable growth' (214) introduces an organic image which continues through the rest of the paragraph. Nature had hitherto *slowly* trained him up 'to stand unpropped' (230) so that he did not need the support of anything, as a plant may need a trellis, for example. The line 'Forced labour, and more frequently forced hopes' (213) suggests that Cambridge was a forcing ground encouraging *quick* growth. Nevertheless, the 'unpropped' plant found itself amidst a 'goodly prospect' (229) and 'leaned by nature' (235) for support towards those 'happy youths' (221) in their 'budding-time' (222), 'the growth/Of life's sweet season' (224–5), and a 'garland of wild flowers' (226). His retrospective view of Cambridge is ambivalent here. He saw in its distraction a danger, yet to have been unmoved by certain beauties within it (youth, hope, health, etc.) would have been to be 'insensible' – emphatically so, 'sodden clay/On a sea-river's bed at ebb of tide' (218–19). The paragraph is asking us to understand (even applaud) what it is also suggesting we reject. This indecisive response is precisely what we are told 'impaired/And shook the mind's simplicity' at that time (215–16). Wordsworth, from his adult standpoint is making us see that Cambridge was in fact forcing him to be more complex. In consequence it is no longer possible for him to make easy judgments. He can see that his heart's sociableness (235–6) was being developed, making him less communicative with Nature but this, he now feels, was a necessary part of his 'education'.

Lines 237–58

As his deeper instincts were untouched by what was going on around him he found it easy to take part in the social life that Cambridge offered without too much thought. The sunless 'Caverns' (246) of his mind contained the source of his real powers and, anyway, he would not have been able to share his 'deeper pleasures' (238) with others as, in spite of trying his hand at a poetry of solitude from time to time (239), he had never given a consciously thoughtful or articulate existence to his innermost feeling (241–2). He uses words which suggest that he thinks of himself as a moral backslider at this time, 'easily' (242), 'slipped' (244), 'sauntered', 'played', 'rioted' (251), 'Unprofitable' (252), 'Drifted' (253), 'lazily' (254). He lacked discrimination, 'Companionships/Friendships, acquaintances, were welcome all' (249–50). When he went sailing on the Cam he did so 'boisterously' (257) and his horse-riding was 'senseless' action (256) though pursued with 'zeal' (255), a word often associated with Puritan devotion (cp. 'duty and zeal dismissed' (333)) but here applied to extravagant behaviour. The appearance of the stars at the end of the paragraph reminds us of loftier ideals neglected and is a quiet afterthought after a statement in which he tells us that at that time he was without 'perhaps . . . one quiet thought' (258).

Lines 259–75

Although superficially social life attracted him most of the time
there were two opposed ways in which his imagination responded
to the thought of 'generations of illustrious men' (263). First, like
the deferential grass which 'yielded' (262) to their steps, he was
pressed upon by a sense of *their* greatness, even a 'dark sense' (268)
that they were 'Of nobler feeling' (269). The ordinary routine of
his daily life (264–7) was disturbed by this sense. Placed against
this (268) was an opposite feeling. The 'great Newton's own
etherial self,/Seemed humbled' (270–1), not by greatness as
Wordsworth was, but by contact 'with tasks/Of life's plain
business' (272–3). So the ordinary daily life which before seemed
disturbed, actually incorporated Newton into it. Newton was not
really 'Of nobler feeling' (269) after all, but humble like himself.
More than this, the dignified 'invested' (272) here means endued
with a moral quality, so that finally we are made to feel that
'plainness' as much as intellectual greatness engendered respect.
Newton's 'daily garb' (273) throws those fashionable trappings
Wordsworth associates with modern Cambridge life into an un-
favourable light. Those 'spiritual men' (269) of a previous age were
'Dictators at the plough' (274) in so far as they worked hard in
breaking new intellectual ground to give the laws that others
follow, but also like Cincinnatus who was ploughing when
summoned to be dictator of Rome, their greatness came from their
very ordinariness. For Wordsworth this was a cause for 'genuine
admiration' (275).

Lines 276–93

He was particularly conscious at Cambridge of his poet-
predecessors, Chaucer, Spenser and Milton. The sublime
remoteness of Spenser ('he is the moon' (281–2)) and of Milton
('Soul awful' (287)), is reduced to familiarity – 'I called
him brother, Englishman, and friend' (283), 'I seemed to see
him here/Familiarly' (288–9). Most lightheartedly of all –

'I laughed with Chaucer' (277). This continued the idea of the previous paragraph. Just as plainness became moral elevation, so here familiarity is idealisation. More lines are devoted to Milton, with whom Wordsworth felt a particular kinship. In the young Poet's mind the 'blind poet' (284) with 'Darkness before' (286) becomes a youth with 'keen eye' and 'courageous look' (292). In the subsequent demise of Milton's youthful optimism into 'darkness', perhaps the mature Wordsworth intends to draw a comparison with himself.

Lines 294–328

In a paragraph which contains much self-ridicule and a deep sense of shame for the indiscretions of youth, he contrasts his drunkenness with Milton's sobriety – 'O temperate bard!' (299). The sonorous Miltonic voice, 'In not a desperate or opprobrious time' (310) contrasts with the grotesque parody of Milton's 'step' (293), 'Ran ostrich-like' (309). 'Upshouldering in a dislocated lump . . . My surplice' (316/18) gives a ludicrous vision of Wordsworth also 'Bounding' (290), but top-heavily, like an ostrich. The 'shallow ostentatious carelessness' (317) with which he donned his surplice shows how the surplice, like all clothing, became a *surplus*. He liked to wear it because it distinguished him from the townsfolk 'On the last skirts of their permitted ground' (321), but he really despised it as an obligatory part of his day (318). It was also a symbol of compulsory chapel which many, including Wordsworth, thought a redundant University tradition. (The bell's 'Cassandra voice' (312) prefigures its end.) The paragraph points out what a later one will do more thoroughly (407–31), that compulsory worship encourages divisions between men and so makes a mockery of religion. The 'pride' with which Wordsworth 'clove . . . through the inferior throng' (319) contrasts with Milton's proper 'pride' (293) while his drunkenness and inegalitarian behaviour were against everything the Republican Milton had stood for. In consequence, he begs forgiveness of both Milton and Coleridge in a genuinely penitent mood for the 'weakness of that hour' (326).

Lines 328–407

The initial lines continue to suggest a slackening of purpose, 'loose indifference, easy likings, aims/Of a low pitch' (332–3). He did not wilfully pursue the wrong track (329–30), but made no effort to devote himself to duty (333). Later, he talks of how 'bred up in Nature's lap' he was 'even/As a spoiled child' (358–9) and the suggestion is that he expected Nature to step in and help him as usual without his having to do so much about it; 'Yet Nature, or a happy course of things,/Not doing in their stead the needful work' (334–5). Cambridge became a sluggish backwater in the river of his life (339–43) and he reached a point of stagnation. The images of marshy vegetation, which looks superficially attractive but is really unsound and unwholesome within, are further examples of how, at Cambridge, showiness concealed reality. Although Cambridge impressed Wordsworth and engendered a 'reverence for the glorious dead' (344), his respect was tempered by a feeling that the academic precincts were a kind of mausoleum, death-marked 'catacombs in which/Perennial minds lie visibly entombed' (345–6). Such a place had been an inspiration to 'rigorous discipline' (348) in the past, but the Poet goes on to say that in its present form it could hardly have been an inspiration to him as a 'spoiled child' (359) of Nature. In its usual sense, spoiling the child is a matter for regret, but here Wordsworth intends us to see that in his case it was something for congratulation. It was better to have been wilful and free. Nature had been his real university tutor and a bad one only in so far as it had *incapacitated* ('ill-tutored') him for the kind of 'captivity' (363) Cambridge demanded. Liberating phrases such as 'rambling like the wind' (359) and 'ranging like a fowl of the air' (362) contrast in their freshness and freedom with the static sense of rotting and entombment previously. The 'lovely forms' (366) with which his mind had been filled did not lead him to reject book-learning ('that were to lack/All sense' (371–2)), but had simply 'left less space' (367) for it. He goes on to envisage ('Yet I could shape/The image of a place' (375–6)) a natural academic community as opposed to the 'deathly' university of his experience. The vision delightfully detains his thoughts as the repetition, 'yet I/Methinks could shape the image of a place' (380–1) suggests. It looks back in its possibilities to when he had been cultivated like a plant in paradise ('trained up . . . /Among sweet garlands' (377–8)) and to when, also, he had, like Adam, been Nature's master, accustomed 'to walk/With Nature magisterially' (379–80). Residence at Cambridge was, in comparison, a fallen condition.

In the ideal 'Republican' (407) university 'seemly plainness' (406) would take its values from the town or ordinary life. The Cambridge 'burghers' were 'plain' (320). Life's 'plain business' (273) was what the 'great Newton' (270) had been *invested* with (272). Later in the Book religious simplicity is symbolised in the 'plain steeples of our English Church' (425) and royal Princes, zealous for knowledge in an earlier, better, University had prized 'plain weeds' (470) when clothes were less important than learning. In Book IV Wordsworth returns to the Lakes to learn piety and simplicity from the 'plain-living people' (204) rather than from the source of learned things, Cambridge.

'Pious' (407) is a vital word. It denotes a particular quality of which Cambridge seemed devoid and which his old dame (see IV 16ff.) possessed in full. Its latter-day sense of devoutly religious is a pale reflection of its original truly Roman and 'Republican' meaning – that is loyalty to the sacred customs and ties of home. Those who in Wordsworth's ideal academic society would 'strip . . . off' their 'trappings' (402) to stand 'abashed/Before antiquity' (402–3) would feel these loyalties most strongly. Antiquity here is seen as an ideal, embodying the high heroisms of truth, simplicity, plainness and piety. It is very near the more contemporary French Republican idealism of which Wordsworth had first-hand knowledge. His conception of an ideal academic community was clearly inspired by the best ideals of revolutionary France as words and phrases elsewhere in the Book suggest. The 'assembly' (308) from which he ran to chapel earlier was 'a festive ring/Of commonplace

convention' (302–3), which, itself, looks forward to the 'ring' of
happy Frenchmen which Wordsworth and Robert Jones joined to
celebrate the feast of the Federation described in Book VI (406ff.).

Lines 407–59

In the Poet's opinion one of the worst forms of 'disguise' where
truth was mocked as well as obscured was the University's insistence on compulsory worship at chapel. If we must have 'Folly and
False-seeming' (410), he says, let us restrict them to academia. To
extend their domain to the Church is to discredit it, not only in
Cambridge, but even ' 'mid remotest village trees' (426). 'Science'
(learning) is descredited, too, (427) because, associated with
hypocrisy and insincerity, the learning of scholars comes under
'Collateral suspicion' (431). Wordsworth goes on to say that he
had raised his expectations of Cambridge (perhaps like the foolish
man of the New Testament who builds on sand) upon a 'basis . . .
Which now before me melted fast away,/Which could not live,
scarcely had life enough/To mock the builder' (436–9). The image
that he had formed was destroyed by reality but the fact of its
destruction does not stop him from dreaming and forming in
manhood another image of what Cambridge could be like. The
natural surroundings of a kind of primeval peaceable kingdom in
the New World are a metaphor for such an academic community
which would be purer even than the best ideals of antiquity. It is
described in terms of an unspoilt Nature (442) and in images of
retirement, retreat, and solitude ('under-coverts' (446); 'shy
rivers' (452); 'cypress-spire' (453)). The culmination of the list of
quiet, ruminating creatures is the pelican sitting 'Upon the
cypress-spire in lonely thought' (453). This clearly stands in
Wordsworth's mind as the natural counterpart to the statue of
Newton ('Voyaging through strange seas of Thought, alone'
(1850, 63)). Furthermore, just as Newton's sublime quiet was
disturbed by the 'loquacious clock' so, too, is the quietness of this
visionary future broken upon by the 'chattering popinjays' (457)
of the present.

Lines 459–91

Wordsworth goes on to imagine the University's great past. We have already been given two visions embodying a Republican ideal and an Edenic primeval ideal. Now we have the Renaissance ideal. In the Cambridge of those days 'Learning, like a stranger come from far,/Sounding through Christian lands her trumpet, rouzed/ The peasant and the king' (475–7). In the pursuit of learning there were no fine social distinctions but 'boys and youths,/The growth of ragged villages and huts' (477–8) were the same as 'illustrious men' (487) in their mutual quest as 'Lovers of truth' (488). Cambridge was then full of scholars for whom knowledge was something to be devoured voraciously; 'crowded, o'er their ponderous books they sate/Like caterpillars eating out their way/ In silence' (464–6). The silent working 'caterpillars' of those days, however, have turned into the flippant 'butterflies' (456) of the previous paragraph, and their 'keen devouring noise' (466) as they ate their remorseless and obscure (467) way through their books has become the pseudo-articulacy of 'chattering popinjays' (457). The asceticism of the dedicated Renaissance scholars (486ff.) was in stark contrast with the 'invitations, suppers, wine, and fruit,/ Smooth housekeeping within, and all without/Liberal' (41–3) of Wordsworth's own experience. Although Milton is not listed with those who 'read . . . By moonshine through mere lack of taper light' (489–91), there may be an intended reference to his induced blindness through just such dedication to study. Wordsworth's reference to his obscured vision, 'We see but darkly/Even when we look behind us' (492–3) at the beginning of the next paragraph, probably follows from this implicit comparison (cp. Milton's 'Darkness before' (286)). Notice how, in contrast to the gaudy clothes of Wordsworth's time, even Princes prized 'plain weeds' (470).

Lines 492–523

Having set out his three notions of the ideal, Republican, Primeval

[71]

and Renaissance, he now checks his idealism. He implies that
memory is selective and that it even seems to be a kind of clothing
when later he says, 'I cannot say what portion is in the truth/The
naked recollection of that time,/And what may rather have been
called to life/By after-meditation' (645–8). He compares himself
to a sailor who might actually bless the wind or his own fear of a
reef for driving him beyond a 'fair enticing island' (498). In
rejecting a vision of the past as a similar kind of paradisial entice-
ment Wordsworth is implying that truth can be falsified by having
too much of an eye on the ideal. He admits that although life at
Cambridge was not perfect a man would be happy indeed to have
experienced only what he did. Although he disliked some things,
there were other things that he *did* like. The tone is one of balance
which prevents the idealistic impulse from distorting the truth. He
is anxious to be fair in his judgments. Although he regretted at that
time the cut-throat competition of ambitious natures which
seemed to be 'low and mean' (514) he is willing now to ascribe this
to 'ignorance of mine,/In part, and want of just forbearance'
(514–15). The judicious balance, however, lends a stronger credi-
bility to his mature opinion, 'yet/My wiser mind grieves now for
what I saw' (515–16). He continues to feel that his life at
Cambridge represented a fall of some kind. There was a general
slackening off and he kept company with 'easy minds/And
pillowy' (529–20). His studies were themselves a 'guise' (507) and
his inclination was to 'travel' (518) with his companions as a
'shoal' (518) drifting with the current of 'The river' (509) of
academic life. His main feeling of regret was that the trivial life he
led caused him to forget the 'pledges interchanged' (522) with his
own 'inner being' (523). One of the most significant episodes in
the next Book will be the making of such a pledge (see IV: 341–5).

Lines 524–63

His lack of taste for the prescribed course reading encouraged him
to turn in a completely undirected and whimsical fashion towards
anything that took his fancy. The 'wild' wood-honey (529) and

'vagrant' fruit (530) suggest self-willed delinquency ('truant', 'Unruly' (529–30)) rather than the tutored or cultivated. The 'fruit' of the first part of the paragraph, unlike the 'better fruits' (562) at the end, suggests the Fall ('vagrant fruit'), while the mood of languid, self-indulgence is to be contrasted with the 'manly' (527) hunt. The 'peeping' about of line 530 suggests timidity and lines 532–5 confirm that withdrawal from more robust failings made him an uncommitted and shadowy figure. Lines 539–43, describing how the deeper parts of his being lay 'locked up' (540), indicate no commitment to his best self either. He tries to find something positive in the Cambridge period, but there is an irony in calling it 'this deep vacation' (542) for he actually had to wait until a holiday (Book IV, 'Summer Vacation') to become the truly 'dedicated spirit' (IV: 344) he should have been during term time. University had, at least, he decides, displayed to him the realities of life as a kind of 'imagery' (555) that better suited his 'visionary mind' (556) than if he had been 'bolted forth' (557) into life itself. As a half-way house between youth and reality it suited his transitional and curiously suspended state of being. The theme of this paragraph is a betwixt and between condition of non-committal supported by phrases like 'midway residence' (554), 'intervenient imagery' (555), and words like 'Hushed' (539), and 'locked' (540). There was no growth (541) just stagnation. He compares himself to an indolent shepherd, so withdrawn into himself that he is out of touch with reality (543–9). The state of suspension was vaguely unhealthy ('sickly appetite' (525)) reminding us of other images of rot and stagnation elsewhere in the Book (see 339–43). Nevertheless he had been able at Cambridge to mature gradually and in consequence been made capable of bearing 'better fruits' (562). That he admits that his life there was 'not given up/To utter waste' (542–3) is consistent with the balanced judgment which he now seems anxious to make.

Lines 564–89

He was intrigued by 'the manners and the ways' (565) of his

teachers. True to his vision of Cambridge, these men were made unreal by trappings and additions, 'arrayed' in the 'livery' of 'good or evil fame' (566–7), 'unscoured', 'grotesque' (574), 'tricked out' (575), 'Objects embossed' (584). They served only to irritate, 'set our minds on edge' (571), whereas Nature's tuition was 'tender' (587) and given with 'sedulous care' (584). These 'grave elders' (574) did not form the deep relationship of love or homely affections which are to be considered in the next Book, but only attachments, like trees 'through the laspse of their infirmity' (576) (another suggestion of decay) giving 'ready place to any random seed/That chuses to be reared upon their trunks' (577–8). The deep-planted seed-time of character in the small boy of Book I (305) contrasts with the student followers or random seeds sticking like parasites with no sustenance of their own. Wordsworth now had two kinds of old age to consider. He was bemused by the dissimilarity between the old dons and the old shepherds of his home county. Yet he saw that they were the same in so far as both were marked by Nature in distinctive ways ('Objects embossed' (584)) for the instruction of youth. The academics 'tricked out' and the shepherds, perhaps deeply lined by weather, were used by 'Nature' (585) to teach youth about life by making possible all kinds of responses (589) to differing object lessons. The irony here is that the distinguished old dons became 'A book of rudiments' (i.e. the very fundamentals of knowledge (583)) held up 'before the eye of youth' in *Nature*'s 'great school' (585–6). Nature was using these old academics for a teaching purpose they were themselves unaware of.

Lines 590–613

Cambridge is now compared to a beautiful silk tapestry whose form and colour change according to the way it catches the light. The immediate source for the image is Spenser's *Faerie Queene* (III: XI: 28),[2] but the sinister and sinful overtones, 'lurking, gleaming . . . woven . . . wily . . . Willingly and unwillingly' (592–5), recall the meanderings of Milton's superficially

beautiful 'wily adder' (*Paradise Lost* IX: 625), and are consistent
with the already noted idea of Cambridge as Fall. Wordsworth
suggests that one would have had to be as subtle as the colours of
the tapestry to survive, and had he 'learned to watch' (596) the
whole process he might have been less inclined to remark upon it
(597–8). As things were, however, he preferred the less subtle
'homely produce' (602) to the 'rarities elaborate' (600) for which
he had not yet acquired a taste (601). Now, from his 'mountain
solitude' (604) he can only smile to himself at the thought of
Cambridge scenes recalled like 'passages and fragments' (605)
from a cheap theatrical production. The unreality theme here
reaches its climax. Wordsworth remembers 'old men,/Old
humourists' (eccentrics (609–10)) who have become 'phantoms'
(612), almost fictional characters, who have never really lived. The
insubstantiality of the place is implicit in the tenuous existence it is
given. As a poet, Wordsworth had a very solid sense of events, and
when he speaks of these old characters as 'having almost in my
mind put off/Their human names' (611–12) he anticipates Book
IV where, in a world of more solid values, he tells us that his old
dame's is a name he *never* will forget (IV: 21).

Lines 614–43

As he draws his account to its conclusion, Wordsworth reiterates
his earlier point that his experiences were 'not wasted' upon him
(622). Again Cambridge is the microcosm where the 'limbs of the
great world' (616) were expressed in 'dwarf proportions' (615).
Cambridge life is seen as a kind of sparring partner who, weaving
about 'in mock fight' (617) would 'hit' (620) him 'this way less,/
More that way' (621–2) and although some of its blows were
'hardly dealt' (618) (i.e. hard hits), they always stopped short of
real injury (619). Cambridge as 'mock fight' gave him a good idea
of what the real contest of life would be like. Quickly changing the
image Wordsworth compares Cambridge to 'A creek of the vast
sea' (626), really no different but affording a protection which the
open sea does not give. His life there presented him with a usefully

scaled-down display of life's realities. The highly inventive list of personifications which follows (630ff.) is a moral allegory where the over-riding impression created is of Cambridge as busy, petty and futile but too dangerous to be ignored. Of particular significance is the figure of 'blind Authority beating with his staff/The child that might have led him' (640–1). In Wordsworth's scheme it is throughout the child who becomes the moral instructor of his elders.

Lines 644–68

He finds himself unable to distinguish the *naked* recollection from what has perhaps been clothed by memory. The very act of remembering is therefore linked to one of the most consistent metaphors in the Book. Memory itself may be a kind of clothing or distortion of truth. What he can be certain of, however, is the 'delight' (648) he felt at that time. Equally, he remembers that Cambridge did no more than touch the surface of his life, 'quickens, pleases, stings' (657). There was no unifying power at work and the jumble of impressions is compared to the effect of walking through a museum with its collection of bits and pieces, science seeming to have broken things apart. The disparaging word 'cabinet' (652) may recall the phrase 'cabinet/Of . . . sensations' (II: 228–9) suggesting artificial compartmentalising. His feelings are not unlike those he had when walking in the confusion of the London streets in Book VII, but there is a difference. There, he says that a potentially 'unmanageable sight' is not 'wholly so to him who looks/In steadiness', who 'sees the parts/As parts, but with a feeling of the whole' (VII: 709–13). It was only, he says, because he had been so used to 'early converse with the works of God' (719) that he kept 'Composure and ennobling harmony' in London (741). At Cambridge, however, he suggests that in this first experience of the wider world he could only see the parts *as* parts, and although most things have since been forgotten, 'Yet something to the memory sticks at last/Whence profit may be drawn in times to come' (667–8). Such a statement anticipates the more specific theory of 'Spots of time' in Book XI where certain episodes beneficial to the mind are recalled because they have been transformed by the more powerful unifying imagination.

Lines 669–72

He was 'Returned' (672) in 'submissive idleness' (669) to his 'native hills' (672). The passivity is important because it suggests that he was now being acted upon rather than acting. The University, it seems, had incapacitated rather than equipped him for life. There had, of course, been many advantages, but for the moment he shows himself as disoriented, unable to give himself to one form of life or another. He needed once again to be dealt with (see I: 371), restored, in fact, reborn. It is perhaps with this latter thought that the unobtrusive 'labouring time' (670) and 'Nine months' (671) are really concerned.

Pattern of thought

The solid and slow-paced world of natural objects and the undeniable strength of his experiences among them, described in Books I and II, give way in Book III to feelings of insecurity and to day-dreams. Cambridge was superficial, fast, and showy and had almost, at times, a fairy-tale unreality. Wordsworth reiterates a conviction that he was not made for such places and dwells at first on his inner life – that under-presence which was his deepest resource and strength. But the contemporary University was little more than a playground for dissolute youth, and without entirely intending it Wordsworth found himself impelled towards sharing their life of 'idleness and joy' (236). The Book is liberally sprinkled with words suggesting his moral slackness, decadence, and decay. It is as though Cambridge is a version of the Fall.

As a contrast to this contemporary condition, Wordsworth dwells on earlier days when plain truth and dedicated learning made Cambridge justly famous. As a direct consequence of his own established values he speculates upon the possibility of a University which would be a kind of natural, prelapsarian community of scholars, more akin to Renaissance ideals of learning and the search for truth. Nevertheless, he is not entirely condemnatory in retrospect, and sees value in his university days if only because they more firmly strengthened his conviction in personal values elsewhere. He derived, too, a sense of the presence of great minds – Milton, Newton.

For Wordsworth, Cambridge was a kind of vacation through which he breezed detachedly, and this Book describing it leads on, ironically, to 'Summer Vacation' (Book IV) where much more memorable 'learning' took place. There is a sense, however, in which the experiences of Book IV are unobtrusively modified by the Cambridge period, so that the return to the Lake District could not be a simple resumption of his life in Books I and II. What it immediately emphasises is a new conviction in the depth of human love. This sentiment had been denied by the social divisiveness and brilliant surfaces of Cambridge life.

BOOK IV

Lines 1–32

The opening lines of this Book are in studied contrast to the opening lines of the previous one. 'A pleasant sight it was' (1) is more promising than, 'It was a dreary morning' (III, 1) and the 'Heights of Kendal' (2) are more exhilarating than the depressing 'flat plains of Huntingdon' (III: 2). Cambridge had been merely 'A creek of the vast sea' (III: 626), narrow and enclosed, whereas the wide prospect now over the 'bed of Windermere' (4) was liberating and spacious. The mind will be expanded, we feel, in the Lakes whereas it had not been in Cambridge. After all, the real 'deep vacation' (III: 542) was *Residence at Cambridge* and so *Summer Vacation* promises to continue Nature's 'great school' (III: 586).

First of all, he felt the thrill of coming home – 'I bounded down the hill' (5). There was a wonderful sense of recognition and belonging after the alienating experience of Cambridge, a heartiness in his 'lusty summons to the farther shore' (6), an outburst of energy and gusto, and a resurgence of feelings in the meeting with his old dame ('Glad greetings' (16); 'some tears' (16); 'Great joy' (29)). This bond remains unbroken for the mature Poet; 'while my heart/Can beat I never will forget thy name' (20–1). Compare this with his fading memory of the university dons to whom he felt no deep ties of affection – 'And, having almost in my mind put off/Their human names' (III: 611–12). Naming is important. Casting our minds back to Book II, we recall that indelible attachment to place and persons which names can signify in 'that old dame/From whom the stone was named' (44–5).

Although we have started out by taking note of the sense of freedom and space, we notice the affectionately diminutive terms used to describe Ann Tyson's (his old dame's) way of life – 'innocent' (23), 'narrow' (24), and 'little' (24). These imply that he brought back to the Lakes a sense of a much broader vision, in spite of the fact that in Book III he had disliked the narrowness of Cambridge. His widened experience seemed to diminish what he found on his return, though affection was deepened, as in the phrase 'narrow precincts, all beloved' (31). So Cambridge *did* change him, but perhaps unexpectedly in ways that were not always to his detriment. He seemed more able, in fact, to see the value of Ann Tyson's simplicity and innocence (20–9), not surprising after the doubtful duplicities of Cambridge. And it is significant that he should turn to her, and not the university dons, as his true teacher – 'she guided me,/I willing, nay – nay – wishing to be led' (56–7). There is the same sense of greatness inherent in littleness to be found in Wordsworth's sonnet beginning 'Though narrow be that old man's cares, and near,/The poor old man is greater than he seems.'[1]

He was also, though more attached to his home, at the same time more detached and apart. 'And many of them seeming yet my own' (32) is slightly elegiac. Something had been lost in that the 'throng of things' (30) seemed to belong to him again, but did not quite completely. So Book IV is not entirely about innocence; whenever there is a re-awakening of the pre-Cambridge feelings of Book II (and his memories take us back a number of times to particular places in that Book) there is always an added feeling of being distanced and separate. In his nostalgia (68–83) and in his impressions of the changing village community as well (181–99), there is something of the detached observer about him.

BOOK IV

Lines 33–67

Detachment, however, does not imply indifference. There was, perhaps to compensate for the elegiac feeling, an effusion of emotion. We have a strong sense of the rootedness of his affections in a particular place and in solid, physical objects (35–7). The 'broad stone table' (37) recalls many festive hours to him and we recall those other stones and tables (II: 45–6; 64–5; 125) which had a power to make the past seem almost tangibly present.

The 'child of mountain birth' (39) refers to himself as much as to the stream and the Poet continues the metaphor until line 55. Looking back now, the parallel between his Cambridge self and the boxed brook (40) seems obvious. He marvels that he had not thought of applying to himself his superior sentiment about the brook when he returned – 'pretty prisoner, are you there!' (48). It might have occurred to him as a student, especially when this 'emblem' (52) was speaking such a clear message, 'to pen down/A satire on myself' (54–5), but he never did. No plainer indication could be given that Book III was intended as that satire upon himself, not merely upon Cambridge, which he had not the self-awareness to write as a student.

'Unceremonious greetings' (61) remind us that, free from Cambridge, ceremony was now put off. Shouting across the field (62) or lake (6), however, was reserved for encounters with the common man. He was more 'constrained' (64) with his school-fellows because they were of his world. This was a change from the spontaneous camaraderie of Book II, the easy friendship of games and horse-riding. There was a loss of innocence which 'pride' (65) and 'shame' (66) remind us of and he carried something of his Cambridge self with him in his 'habiliments' (66) and 'gay attire' (67). At the same time we must not overlook the fact that Book IV is full of images of caring, purity ('snow-white church' (13)) and simple domestic attachment, as against Book III's images of strife, ambition, parasitism, and rot.

Though the season is summer, moreover, images of springtime (94, 126, 186) suggest new growth and new beginnings. The 'dawning, even as of another sense' (224) and the 'Magnificent' dawn itself (330) also continue the theme of new departures in his life despite the burden of his Cambridge self.

Lines 68–83

Sitting down at the old table was far from being the commonplace domestic routine it had once been; for the returning student, it was a keen delight (68). Lying down in his 'accustomed bed' (73) was much more than the thoughtless end to the day of Book II when 'to bed we went/With weary joints and with a beating mind' (17–18). It was now a more conscious 'joy' (72) because of the memories it evoked.

Return to a setting, here simply his bedroom, which was indelibly associated with childhood impressions, triggered off a memory submerged by the Cambridge period. This points forward to the 'spots of time' concluding Book XI when a return to a particular place calls up and intensifies past sensations . . . 'feeling comes in aid/Of feeling' (XI: 325–6).

Notice the Chinese-box effect. The Poet remembers himself as a student and the student remembered his childish self years before watching the moon in the tree through that same bedroom window. Moving back in time to the Book II period, a moment of almost nursery-rhyme romance is recalled. Lines 81–3 describe the 'rock-a-bye-baby' appeal of the child's naive illusion that the moon was being blown to and fro by the wind. The phrase 'fixed eyes' (81) describes his stare of reverie. We imagine the student's eyes similarly fixed, as he remembers, and we are returned like him to that visionary world in which the moon had seemed present in the vale (see II: 195–202).

Lines 84–120

The time referred to in this paragraph is also pre-Cambridge ('when first/The boyish spirit flagged' (91–2)). The passage is a self-satire upon his early poetic eccentricities. A mock-heroic tone introduces the 'rough terrier of the hills' (86). He was 'by ancient right/Our inmate' (85–6), having a right to the hospitality due to an old and faithful retainer. The youthful Wordsworth, as his implied lord, was well served by him in the comic episode which follows. Notice the word 'inmate' establishing again that feeling of belonging so absent from the society of Cambridge. Replacing the 'boyish spirit' (92) was an adolescent, self-conscious mood of introspective melancholy. He was to be found 'affecting private shades/Like a sick lover' (95–6). Even the word 'poesy' (95), as a somewhat pretentious preference over the simpler word 'poetry', catches the boy's affected diction.

There was an inner turmoil and tingling excitement – 'Along my veins I kindled' (93). Note, too, the over-excited agitation and almost uncomfortable intensity expressed in 'the stir,/The fermentation and the vernal heat/Of poesy' (93–5); 'fermentation', especially, suggests intoxication as well as the yeasty working of a new poetic energy.

The dog was faithful, but amusingly bewildered by its master's oddities – 'Tired, and uneasy at the halts I made' (100). The phrase 'toil of verse' (102) suggests fruitless plodding and 'Great pains and little progress' (103) is self-mocking. The image in the boy's mind rising up 'like Venus from the sea' (105) points forward to a later revelatory rising-up in Book V (471–2), the dead man from the lake. This kind of sudden encounter with solitary figures occurs often. For example, the soldier at the end of this Book makes the same kind of surprising appearance. Nevertheless, there is intentionally self-mocking exaggeration in the application of this great classical revelation to his own youthful image-making. The ridiculous onrush of affection for the 'terrier' (86), 'stormy joy' (107), is a come-down from the sublimely inspirational 'Venus from the sea' (105), a comic descent from the Goddess Venus to the earth (terrier – Fr. terre = earth). The same pattern appears in the comedy of lines 110–20. After playing the inspired poet 'like a river murmuring' (110), he hurriedly hushed his voice (116–17), anxious for his reputation, unwilling to risk 'piteous rumours' (119) of being 'crazed in brain' (120).

Lines 121–80

He now rediscovered the same walks in his first summer vacation from Cambridge, but in a new mood of self-discovery and self-awakening. This paragraph is thus in deliberate antithesis to the previous one. Awkward affectation was dispelled and replaced by serenity (125), so dispensing with any further need for satire or self-mockery from the mature Poet. Certain words and phrases mark the contrast and the move forward – from 'vernal heat/Of poesy' (94–5), suggesting oppressive passion, to the gentler 'returning spring' (126); from 'fermentation' (94), suggesting intoxication and yeasty agitation, to 'sober hour' (134). No longer moody, restless, and erratic, he was now 'steady, calm, contemplative' (131). Whereas before he had hurriedly hushed his soulful outpourings in embarrassment, he now bared his soul (140–2) which gently 'Put off her veil, and, self-transmuted, stood/Naked as in the presence of her God' (141–2).

There are Biblical echoes here. In the process of spiritual renewal spoken of by St Paul, divestment is the operative metaphor. In the man whose soul turns to God, the veil upon his heart 'shall be taken away' (Corinthians II 3: 16). At Cambridge, Wordsworth had acquired a false front represented, as we have seen, by numerous clothes (new suits, gowns, surplices). That process was now reversed and there was a sense of liberation and release from an old, corrupt self. Release came in more ways than one, as lines 143–8 explain. First, the obscurity veiling his earlier weakness (145) and weariness (148) was taken away, so that he now recognised these hitherto 'unacknowledged' failings (148). Instantaneous with this clarity of insight came 'restoration' (146).

When he says (150) that he was pleased with what he saw in himself, although self-examination had revealed 'little' of any worth, he means that now vast scope for improvement became possible. Lines 150–2 express the feeling typical of moments of religious conversion – a sense of empty openness, of being personally worthless and so ready for complete renewal. All this gave rise to a euphoric sense of release.

We must take careful note that his soul was 'self-transmuted'

(141) and was only 'as in the presence of her God' (142). That is to say, 'I' – and not God – 'took/The balance in my hand and weighed myself' (148–9). The soul herself actually possessed a 'godlike power' (156) for Wordsworth and so emphasis is upon her self-sufficiency. We may notice, indeed, that 'knocking at the door/Of unacknowledged weariness' (147–8) echoes the *Revelation of St. John the Divine* (3:20): 'Behold, I stand at the door, and knock: if any man hear my voice, and open the door, I will come in to him . . .'. The point of Wordsworth's allusion, however, is not direct reference to Christ, but to echo a passage describing the welcoming in of a new self.

The soul's qualities are exhaustively described; they are creative and inspirational. 'Soul' and 'imagination' are interchangeable terms in *The Prelude* (see XIII: 65). Feelings of emotional 'fulness' (139) gave rise to a sense of his soul pervading and reviving his mind (155). Its power 'spreads abroad' (160) and into all areas of a man's life (162–6). The insight which afforded the Poet a sense of possible glory finally won in his life's work (165–6) was that this pervasive 'pastoral quiet' (164) could enter not only into 'holiday repose' (163), but also into the 'heart/Of amplest projects' (164–5). It was, we remember, in Book I (1–271) that Wordsworth seemed able to see his life only in terms of either completely idle 'pastoral quiet' or a total dedication to 'amplest projects'. He now hoped that a marriage of the two would succeed.

Echoes of Book I emphasise a return of this sense of enchanting peace; 'in a wood I sate me down' (167) recalls 'a green shady place where down I sate/Beneath a tree' (I: 71–2) and 'amplest projects' (165), on the other hand, recalls that heroic ambition to produce 'some work/Of glory' (I: 85–6). This paragraph records an impulse to effect a synthesis between these opposing tendencies. And so we feel now that the 'hopes' (152) will be fulfilled, in contrast especially to those of Book III ('My spirit was up, my thoughts were full of hope' (16)) which at Cambridge turned out to be disappointments. The phrase 'deepest sleep' (157) refers to the Cambridge experience, recalling the soporific line in Book III, 'I was the dreamer, they the dream' (28).

In contrast to this sleepiness, we conclude here in a mood of

BOOK IV

hypersensitive and disturbing alertness in which the wind played
tricks with him (172–80). It records again that odd uneasiness
which the Poet had in moments especially of quiet contemplation
(167). His thoughts were something like, 'Is it just the dog, or is
there something else (a presence) in the wood? Is the sound
explicable or am I being haunted?'

Lines 181–99

Following on from the theme of spiritual renewal, this paragraph
records a new sense of the 'freshness' (181) he found in 'human
life' (182). Its spring-time imagery is entirely appropriate in a
Book which abounds in accounts of new beginnings – such as the
'dawning, even as of another sense' (224), the actual magnificent
dawn (330–9) and the personal dedication to poetry (340–5).

The horticultural metaphor is central, expressing the young
man's sense of teeming fertility and growth ('growing girls'
(197)) in the human community itself. Wordsworth's eye for the
girls is as much exercised here as in a later paragraph (325–7). The
sense of his home village, after Cambridge, as a burgeoning garden
(185–7), leads naturally on to the products of human fertility, the
'pale-faced babes' (194) who had become 'rosy prattlers' (196);
their paleness had blossomed into rosiness. The old man, now
presumably dead, was simply thought of as someone who 'had
been used to sun himself' (193). 'Now empty' (194) is not an
occasion for mourning because *all* changes, even this one, are
incorporated into the overall sense of change as growth. Notice,
too, that beauty never seems to be lost, but merely 'filched' (197)
from one girl to be conferred upon another. The beauty itself
remains, to blossom elsewhere in new growth.

Lines 200–21

Everything, in fact, was seen with more than mere recognition and
a resurgence of old affection; it was seen afresh with 'another eye'

(200) which here amounts to an amused but affectionate detachment. A 'delicate' (202) humour which was love moved him to smiles (201), neither patronising nor contemptuous, when looking at the woodman, shepherd, or his 'grey-haired dame' (208). This humour was also 'knowledge' (205). It is as though, having more the measure of his old dame now (and it is a diminutive one), he yet loves her the more for it. There is none of the satirical bite of Book III's clothes imagery in his affectionate description of her Sunday best. He conveys its odd appearance of old-fashioned grandeur in his description of it as a 'mantle such as Spanish cavaliers/Wore in old time' (212–13). The phrase 'monumental trim' (210) perfectly conveys the disparity of grand and little, and 'work/Of state' (209–10) suggests the solemnity of her public appointments from her own point of view. Her complete lack of real solemnity, however, appears in the quiet humour of her falling asleep upon the Bible (220–1). A new appreciation of her worth ('thoughts unfelt till now' (218)) lay behind the humour. The young man 'loved the book' (220) – *the* book, the Bible – when, used as a pillow, its reading was neglected. Her 'piety' (216) did not consist in the sophistication of book-learning or Bible-reading, a lesson it was important to learn after the emptiness of these pursuits as practised at the University. She might be intellectually 'shallow' (216), but her piety possessed a purity which was more valuable; it was, as the stream-image simply puts it, 'clear' (216).

Lines 222–46

Finally, in this inventory of new insights and feelings, he singles out what seems to be the creation of 'another sense' (224). It had the force of revelation suggested by such phrases as 'Distinctly manifested' (223) and 'opened on me' (231), and it seemed like a new beginning, a 'dawning' (224) or 'new-born feeling' (233). The distinctly religious tone of these phrases, however, serves to herald a more *human* and less *spiritual* state. Wordsworth defines his new 'sense' as a 'human-heartedness about my love/For objects' (225–6) and he contrasts it with the pure, self-sufficient bliss which a 'blessèd spirit/Or angel' (228–9) might experience. He seems to be saying that now his love of Nature was less purely ecstatic and so less 'private' (227) or visionary than it once was; we recall, here, the 'bliss ineffable' of Book II (419) and this is the 'love/Enthusiastic', the 'delight and joy' of the seventeen-year-old referred to in lines 245–6. Wordsworth is making precise comparisons with earlier emotional stages. He recalls, too, an even earlier period when Nature had seemed 'strong,/Deep, gloomy . . . and severe' (242–3); the earlier boyhood experiences of Book I, such as boating, come to mind. Now, aged eighteen, such feelings of severity in Nature were replaced by feelings of love. The whole universe seemed humanised, as though it were man's natural home, so that the very constellations ('those fair Seven' (237)) were now seen to be 'Acquaintances of every little child' (238) and Jupiter, his birth-star, was now thought of as 'my own belovèd star' (239). The stars seemed to belong 'in their old haunts' (235) in his home valley, like the moon in Book II (196). Immersed as he had been in his private world, all awareness of time and change in Books I and II had been held outside, or at least on the edge of, consciousness. Now, however, 'change' (232) gently intruded and so 'regret' (232, and see also 75), a quietly elegiac sense, was naturally felt. This sense gradually spread outwards to affect the natural world (233–42) and it perhaps qualified that ecstatic apprehension of a vibrant 'one life' (II: 430) felt earlier. His feelings for Nature were now neither fearful nor ecstatic, so much as 'tender' (242), because humanising 'shades of mortality' (240) fell everywhere.

Lines 247–304

We now embark (in a metaphorical boat) upon a long paragraph. It deals with the difficulty of seeing the truth clearly. Its first twenty-two lines, constituting a single sentence, centre upon the ambiguous process of remembering. The companionship upon a difficult journey (tracing the Poet's life) of Book II (1–3) and that strenuous uphill struggle of understanding and explication also in Book II (287–90) have become a leisurely boat-trip; a figure, representative of both writer and reader (the 'we' of lines 262–8), leans over the side of a 'slow-moving boat' (248), 'solacing himself' (249) – for exactly *what* becomes clear later in the paragraph – by staring at objects on the lake floor. This diversion is attended by a pleasant optical perplexity (254). It is often difficult to distinguish between the landscape reflections on the lake's surface (255–6) and the actual objects at the bottom of the lake (256–8). Sometimes (259), one's own reflection gets in the way. Similarly, looking back through memory, we are unable to distinguish our present self and circumstances from that past self (the lake's depths) on which we are trying to focus. Memory, however, has not so much been bedevilled by this ambiguity up to now in Book IV as actually sweetened by it (261). The pleasant task of trying to sort out the ambiguities leads one to linger (268).

Now this apparent aside upon memory forms the transition, in this Book, from the preceding sections about improvements in his life and character to the following lines about moral failings. The leisurely look at his earlier self has been perhaps too 'solacing' (249) and so, over-selective. The other side of the coin is now to be looked at and the fuller implications inherent in the ambiguity of his experiences are to be pursued. The expression 'human heart-edness' (225) must not blind us to the 'heartless chace/Of trivial pleasures' (304–5). A deepening of love (undeniably strong as the repeated insistence upon it implies (271 and 272)) must not solace our attention so as to exclude its opposite, the superficial 'swarm/Of heady thoughts' (272–3), his appetite for feasting and dancing (274). In this way, the apparently diversionary sentence upon memory helps to introduce a change of attitude to his past.

Far from 'soft' (266) or 'alluring' (265), the tone becomes openly condemnatory; 'inner falling-off' (270) suggests sinfulness; 'gawds' (273) and 'a badge, glossy' (276) imply that his pastimes were showy, superficial, and devoid of integrity. His lack of 'zeal' (279), 'which had every day been mine' (280) suggests a lost possibility, rather than an actual slackening in behaviour, because 'had' may have the subjunctive sense of 'might have'. The tense of the verb shimmers from past perfect to conditional as one reads. So the ambiguity is the same as before in the reflection. A clear perspective on the past becomes perplexity. Was the 'zeal' of line 279 a reality now vanished or merely a remote possibility, something which had never happened at all? Notice, too, how lines 284–5 ('societies/That were, or seemed, as simple as myself') continue the note of ambiguity suggested by the reflection image. Simplicity itself seemed to have disappeared.

The stern phrase, 'these vanities,/And how they wrought' (288–9), suggests that sin was actively working upon him. Furthermore, the word 'wrought' (cp. lines 93–4) is a term for fermentation, appropriately implying a yeasty seething and agitation. 'Contagious air' (290) which was 'Unknown among these haunts in former days' (291) may imply some corruption brought with him from Cambridge, but it more likely refers to a new influence in this old environment. Even the paradise of the Lakes seemed momentarily to have darkened and fallen from grace, even as he had. This increased the burden of a corrupt self represented by the Cambridge 'garments' (292) which parasitically preyed upon his strength. The use of this imagery implies a stepping-back into the atmosphere of Book III after the earlier divestment (142). The 'stream of self-forgetfulness' (294) in classical myth was the river Lethe – the implication being that Wordsworth *wished* to die to his old self (in the Pauline sense) but could not. Man is either going to measure up to his potential dignity (297), the Poet asserts, or not. If not, he will sink to a bestial level (302). The notion of man as a 'senseless idol' (304) emphasises his capability for emptiness, but also points up the liberation from it in the next paragraph. Images of obscured sight (295–6) and darkness (301) are to be dispelled in the flood of illumination to follow (330–9).

The whole paragraph, then, is about the difficulties of seeing – either in himself looking back, or in his early self-seeking truth. Reason, his mind's eye, was as 'perplexed' (295) then as the Poet sometimes finds himself now. It is not surprising, therefore, to find him looking at the same events from different viewpoints, in order to set right the distortions. At this point in his argument, he judges his early love of feasting and dancing to have diverted him from his nobler self, the high heroism of his 'habitual quest' (278). This view is not final, as the next paragraph demonstrates. One view is set against another to prepare for a final synthesis (in this case, the paragraph lines (346–359)). The whole sense of contagion, sin, and irreligion which the mature Poet deploys his rhetoric to produce here, must be seen as a bleak comment on his past which, in the next paragraph, he reverses.

Lines 304–45

Nevertheless, the regretful tone continues for a while. The Poet is at first unable to see any advantage gained from his bright social life (307–10). He dwells mournfully upon what might have been or should have been (311–13). At this point, however, he checks the tendency to censure his earlier self. Three important lines suddenly arrest the negative sense of loss and regret. 'And yet, in chastisement of these regrets,/The memory of one particular hour/Doth here rise up against me' (314–16). Paradoxically, the memory that 'rises up' in revelatory fashion chastises the Poet's actual impulse to chastise! And so the sternly judging tone of the preceding paragraph, and the beginning of this one, is reversed. It seems that there is something positive to say about feasting and dancing after all, and the following episode even proves that they can serve a noble purpose. Without the 'dancing, gaiety and mirth' (320) of the night of rural festivities, he would never have gone on to experience at daybreak the major turning-point in his career as a poet. There is an easy continuity from the heady euphoria of the festivities to the sublime exhilaration of the ensuing sunrise.

The 'festal company of maids and youths,/Old men and matrons' (317–18) is a meeting of that rural community of old and young which appeared at the beginning of Book II. Whereas there we saw it in an innocent mood, here we meet it in one of unrestrained enjoyment and amorous excitement. 'Slight shocks of young love-liking' (325) lead on to priapic implications in such phrases as 'Spirits upon the stretch' (324) and 'mounted up like joy' (326). Physical and visual titillation are there in 'tingled through the veins' (327) and 'glancing forms' (322). There is no censure in the Poet's tone; 'promiscuous' (318), we must remember, means 'varied' or 'disorderly' and had not acquired its modern pejorative sense in Wordsworth's day. The description simply evokes an effervescent sense of physical excitement which distinctly uplifts and stimulates rather than morally degrades. In the preceding paragraph the emphasis was on 'falling-off' (270) or descent, but in this one it is on mounting up (326) and the emotional ascent continues to the end.

The cock-crow (328) heralds a momentous event and the dawn's glory, equally auspicious, signifies that new beginning towards which the argument of this Book has been moving. The first words to describe the dawn ('Magnificent' (330); 'memorable pomp' (331)) suggest almost a hero's welcome, a visual flourish of trumpets, and this is continued in the landscape's outburst of joy expressed in 'The sea was laughing at a distance' (333). The euphoric superlative of line 332 leads on to the description of something like a celestial vision with the scene 'drenched in empyrean light' (335). The physically solid mountains acquired the lightness of clouds (334) so that the landscape seemed on the edge of dissolving into pure light.

Below the high-flown 'pomp' of the mountain-dawn, there was a smaller scale one in the valleys (336–7). From magnificence we descend to 'sweetness' (337) and finally to the humble reality of 'labourers going forth into the fields' (339). The scene takes in the vast and the small, incorporating the celestial and the humble; it seems appropriately representative of Wordsworth's poetic vision in the years to come.

Finally, in a heart-felt address to his fellow-poet (340) he tells how, in response to this scene, he became Nature's priest, a 'dedicated spirit' (344). The vows made for him (342) suggest a kind of ordination. The note of hollowness and irreligion ('sense-less idol' (304)) which concluded the previous paragraph is dispelled in the emotional and spiritual plenitude expressed in the statement 'to the brim/My heart was full' (340–1). The empyrean light, liquidly drenching (335) the landscape, was Nature's gift of grace. Its reception by the young Poet is expressed in the passive way in which vows were made for him (341–2). We have that sense of a deeper or better self to which he must now make a particular effort to remain true (343–4).

Such an epiphany as this one makes us particularly aware of the desolation of his uncreative mood in Book I (238–71). It is in the light of this joyful singling out that the regretful phrase, 'Was it for this . . . ?' (271) makes forceful sense. The ordination references (341–5) recall too that in Book I his poet's vocation was also defined as a priestly one. 'To the open fields I told/A prophesy; poetic numbers came/Spontaneously, and clothed in priestly robe/My spirit, thus singled out, as it might seem,/For holy services' (I: 59–63).

Lines 346–59

These lines are a synthesis of the opposed views previously presented of the young man. He was a divided being, 'grave and gay,/Solid and light, short-sighted and profound,/Of inconsiderate habits and sedate' (347–9). Morally split, he was a creature of ambiguities who on the one hand 'knew the worth of that which I possessed' (351), yet who 'slighted and misused' (352) it. This whole section, in its judicious awareness of contradictions, reaches a more balanced judgment than the writer's bitter regrets led him to in the earlier section (268–304). We are referred back to its pestilence image, the 'swarm/Of heady thoughts jostling each other' (272–3); picking it up again, he now considers that this 'swarming' (353) of 'thoughts/Transient and loose' (353–4) did not actually deprive him of his deeper singleness of purpose (357–9). 'Conformity' (357), however, suggests that he needed to be *made* to toe the line and the following incident with the soldier does indeed hit him with a shock of admonition. There is a sense in which the argument of the paragraph, with its resolution of opposing tendencies, concludes the Book, and lines 356–9 read like a triumphant climax.

Lines 360–99

Lines 360–2, in their casualness, take away something from the grand finale of the preceding four, i.e. 356–9. This is significant, in that conclusions are less absolute than they seem to be, process and growth being paramount. Beginning (unexpectedly) anew is important in this Book. The soldier experience to follow is an instance of those 'primitive hours' (355) just referred to, but the Poet looks beyond its present purpose in his assurance that he will soon 'pass to other themes' (362). With his eye on the far distance in this way, Wordsworth gives us a sense of his expansive concerns.

Lines 363–99 describe the receptive mood of reverie which prepared him for the dream-like apparition of the soldier soon to follow. Moonlit nights, with their strange quality of a 'deeper quietness' (367), are always imaginatively exciting times in *The Prelude*. We start out with a journey image which points forward. 'I slowly mounted up a steep ascent' (370) looks towards that final mounting to revelation in the Snowdon passage (Book XIII: 1ff.). On the other hand, the 'road's wat'ry surface' (371) which 'glittered in the moon' (372) so that it 'seemed before my eyes another stream' (373), recalls that pathway of liquid light in the wake of his rowing-boat (Book I: 391–4) which there, as here, led to an apparition. The effort of mounting up a 'steep ascent' (370), moreover is posited against the too easy (moral) road down. 'Creeping with silent lapse' (374) has rich Miltonic echoes of the Fall ('lapse') and the Serpent ('creeping'), which accentuate Wordsworth's contrary upward movement to righteousness and his Good Samaritan activities with the soldier.

Now follows a precise description of his state of reverie. The senses were 'listless' (379) and 'Quiescent' (380), so that concentration upon his surroundings faltered – only near objects on the road occasionally intruded themselves upon his attention (378–9). The visual alertness needed for appreciation of distant prospects (383) was lacking due to mental exhaustion (381). His attention was inward rather than outward, a mood in which there was a spontaneous image-flow from the subconscious into the conscious mind – 'beauteous pictures now/Rose in harmonious imagery; they rose/As from some distant region of my soul/And came along like dreams' (392–5). This trance-like state between waking and sleeping in which his body 'from the stillness' drank in 'restoration like the calm of sleep' (386–7), is one upon which the Poet still places a particular value as his apostrophe 'O happy state!' (392) makes clear. The reverie was somehow supported and balanced by his physical delight in walking (385–8). Quiescence and activity conspired to produce a half-way consciousness in which 'animal delight' (397) was 'Obscurely mingled' (396) with an introspective dream-like concentration on beautiful pictures in the mind's eye. This state made him especially receptive to the ghostly encounter to come.

Lines 400–63

There is a dramatic contrast between the Poet's movement (399) and the abruptly static quality of the soldier, emphasising how the Poet had definitely come up against something. Notice, in particular, how the soldier's form 'Kept the same steadiness' (424), how 'His shadow lay, and moved not' (425), how 'he remained/Fixed to his place' (429–30). Even after the slight gesture of salutation he 'then resumed/His station as before' (439–40) and did not even seem *equipped* to move, having neither 'staff,/Nor knapsack' (416–17). The appearance of this arresting figure may be compared to that of the beggar in Book VII: 608ff.

He is also similar to the dead man in Book V who, pulled from Lake Esthwaite, 'bolt upright/Rose with his ghastly face, a spectre shape' (V: 471–2). The soldier seemed similarly spectral, even corpse-like, as 'his mouth/Shewed ghastly in the moonlight' (410–11). Adding to the sense that he was a figure appearing almost from a realm of imagination and Romance, he was like a giant, 'A foot above man's common measure tall' (406).

There was a strange intermediate quality in his behaviour and appearance, seemingly only half-alive. This is enhanced by the use of certain ambivalent phrases, such as 'Half-sitting and half-standing' (413), and 'neither slow nor eager' (442). As a wanderer, too, he was half in and half out of the human family. No longer a soldier, he was now a liminal figure, socially betwixt and between.

His situation as a discharged soldier reminds us of those who are 'in the world/Neglected and ungratefully thrown by/Even for the very service they had wrought' (I: 544–6). We recall the contrasting situation of the boy Wordsworth's 'thick-ribbed army' (I, 544) of cards in Book I who were *not* discarded, but 'husbanded through many a long campaign' (547). The Poet's intention here, as in the card-playing episode, is to stress care and concern. The comfortable community hard by (450–1) is carefully juxtaposed to the homeless wanderer and, though not explicitly stated in so many words, there is a clear sense in which the solitary man will put the values of that community to the test. In this way, the soldier is a bit like Coleridge's Ancient Mariner. His aura of 'desolation' (418) is similar and the situation of young Wordsworth not unlike that of the wedding-guest. Wordsworth, after all, has encountered here an example of suffering and endurance, a sobering admonition to his own wedding-guest-like love of feasting, dancing, music and cheerful company. The soldier even had the mariner's emaciated look – 'lank and lean' (407) and told, like him, a tale about the tropics (446).

The young Poet acted as a kind of intermediary between the soldier and the nearby community, confidently asserting that the labourer living in the wood (perhaps one of those we have already glimpsed 'going forth into the fields' at dawn (339)) would provide food and shelter 'with a ready heart' (458). The soldier's stooping to the ground (459–60) revealed that he did have a 'traveller's staff' (461) after all. No longer static, he surprisingly appeared capable of movement.

Lines 464–504

As he began to move, the Poet's initial reaction of 'fear' (421) returned and he could hardly control it – 'I beheld/With ill-suppressed astonishment his tall/And ghastly figure moving at my side' (466–8). His sudden appearance during the Poet's mood of reverie (402) had made him seem almost a product of imagination – and he continued to have a half-supernatural, ghastly quality (411,468). To some extent this awesomeness was mitigated by his human weakness. 'Solemn and sublime/He might have seemed, but . . ./There was . . . a tone/Of weakness' (473–6). The soldier was half-human and half ghostly, an ambivalence which was disturbing. The Poet's reaction vacillated between fear and compassion (421).

Lacking in energy and remote in manner (475–6), the soldier was only *just* of this world. He seemed to have receded from that full involvement in life, that energy and gusto, which the young Poet has been so full of in this Book. As such, he was most in need of a welcome back into the human community and it was, appropriately, the young man's task to effect it. The theme of belonging with which the Book began thus culminates in this episode, with its echoes of the Good Samaritan. Even such ghastly figures as the discharged soldier are to be brought back into the fold. Wordsworth left his 'comrade' (488) – note the respectful use of this military word for 'companion', suggesting a new bond of friendship – with some practical advice about how to conduct his journey, encouraging him to speak out and ask for help (489–92). The soldier replied laconically with an utterance of impressive solemnity. 'He said, "My trust is in the God of Heaven/And in the eye of him that passes me" ' (494–5). At this quietly dramatic juncture, we feel that all the sacred values of community and home, the firm but simple pieties celebrated at the Book's beginning, need someone such as the soldier to prove them truly whole.

The soldier's final utterance was more energetic than his previous one (494) – 'in a voice that seemed/To speak with a reviving interest/Till then unfelt, he thanked me' (498–500). The key-word is 'reviving'; we end with a final renewal, in this Book of new beginnings. The young Poet, in engendering this response from the soldier, has drawn him back into the human world of warmth and feeling, thawing his almost deathly immobility and perhaps forging another link in the community. After so much

[97]

spiritual renewal, the most important initiation for the young Poet has been into the purely human.

Pattern of thought

Book IV begins and ends on the theme of belonging and inclusiveness. Cambridge, as described in Book III, had merely scratched the surface of Wordsworth's attention, but it had made him alert to the human values it so strenuously denied. Paradoxically, the narrowness he accused it of had the effect of broadening his vision and this Book is about spiritual renewal and conscious reminiscence. His conviction in himself as one 'singled out' (1: 62), always beneath the surface in Cambridge days, is in this Book vindicated in the epiphany so beautifully described in 315–45.

His feelings were now less self-centred and less confined to moments of strong emotion and sensation as in Books I and II. They were more tender, humane, and outward-looking, to include the common man and the outcast. Going along with these feelings was a new awareness, too, of change and of mortality in contrast to his perception (in Book II) of the pure living energy of the 'one life' (430). All these emotions look towards the statements and attitudes of Wordsworth's maturer vision e.g. 'the still, sad music of humanity' (*Tintern Abbey*) and 'Love of Nature leading to love of Mankind' (*Prelude* VIII). Book IV also offers us ambiguous perspectives upon the past, traced in all their perplexity and finally resolved. The Poet's own divided viewpoint very much mirrors the divisions in the student, so that we sense a new complexity in the younger Wordsworth which brings him closer to the Poet.

BOOK V

Lines 1–48

The previous books, in spite of the ostensibly educational element in the titles of three of them, have looked 'Upon the speaking face of earth and heaven' (12) as 'prime teacher' (13) and not at book learning at all. Education has meant education 'by beauty and by fear' (I: 306), and it might be assumed that in this Book Wordsworth is going to make amends for his omissions by considering the value of culture in his life. The paragraph shows, however, that what emerges much more clearly from his considerations is a frightening sense of the impermanence of art in the face of the much more enduring and ultimately alien powers of Nature.

The Book opens in a tone of moderated 'sadness' (10) which he expresses, first of all, for the general condition of mankind, 'it grieves me for thy state, O man' (3), even though this is to some extent a sadness which he can ignore, 'that weight . . . /I charm away' (6–7). What really 'fuels' his sadness (10), it will soon become clear, is a sense that the great achievements of the intellect, 'Things worthy of unconquerable life' (19), are very precarious possessions and terribly vulnerable to destructive forces. Wordsworth reminds us that up to this point he has been writing of that 'intercourse' (13) made possible between man and Nature through the 'Sovereign Intellect' (14) which has 'diffused/A soul divine'

[99]

(15–16) through the visible appearance ('bodily image' (15)) of things. A similar intercourse between man and man is made possible by books. Yet it is the very fragility of books as the embodiments of intellect which makes him inevitably feel that all man's intellectual achievements may at some future time come to perish. As this thought takes hold, a mounting sense of anxiety becomes prominent. Thoughts of the next life where there will be no need for books ('such garments' (23)) to clothe the immortal spirit give 'Tremblings of the heart' (21). In that existence there will be a naked confrontation with eternal truths, an awe-inspiring, unimaginable state. As long as he lives 'a child of earth' (24), however, man will have another kind of fear – that he may have to survive ('Abject, depressed, forlorn, disconsolate' (27)) the destruction of books. This situation makes him, in Shakespeare's paradoxical phrase, almost ' "weep to have" ' (25) what he fears to lose (see Sonnet 64). There follows a terrifying prospect of world destruction, a vision shared by many contemporaries of Wordsworth (see e.g. the paintings of John Martin, 1789–1854), where earthquake (29), or fire (30), or (as in the next paragraph) deluge, bring all things to an apocalyptic conclusion.[1]

Wordsworth's catastrophe would not mean the end of absolutely everything. He talks of how the 'living presence' (33) would manage to re-establish itself in a new dawn of the world. But tragically, the 'consecrated works of bard and sage' (41) would most likely perish. In a question full of puzzled anguish he seeks to know why the mind should not have some more substantial element to 'stamp her image on' (45). Instead, it must rely upon such frail 'shrines' (48) as books, a term reminding us not only of their precious contents but also of their susceptibility to destruction.

Book V, then, begins quietly but by the end of the first paragraph shows its author to be profoundly disturbed. Those natural forces already described in earlier books are here being seen as possibly destructive on a universal scale. The vision is distinctly modern in that Wordsworth seems to conjure up the aftermath of something like a nuclear holocaust. The world's new dawn would break, but it would probably be in a changed form, e.g. 'kindlings like the morning' (35). Against his 'steadiest mood of reason' (1), therefore, he has placed another kind of thought, one which, he writes, is only with him 'sometimes' (28) and which is certainly not conducive to tranquillity – namely, that ultimately destructive forces will prevail. Against them books as fruits of 'hard thought' (8) or 'adamantine holds of truth' (38) will be very frail. If one looks again at the opening line of this Book one can see that the phrase, 'Even in the steadiest mood of reason' carried a suggestion of uneasiness in it from the start. It is as though the mood of reason is, at best, unstable and can only be 'held' against what by the end of this paragraph has become sheer fright.

Lines 49–139

Paragraph one's mood of reason is now replaced by its opposite – a dream. In the edition of 1850 Wordsworth says that it was his own dream, but in this version it was a friend's (49). He was prompted to tell it by Wordsworth giving voice to his fear (50). The friend (perhaps Coleridge) answered 'with a smile that in plain truth/ 'Twas going far to seek disquietude' (51–2). 'With a smile' is ironic because the truth, it turns out, is not so plain. The friend 'confessed' (53) that although ''Twas going far' to think about such things, he too 'at sundry seasons had himself/Yielded to kindred hauntings' (54–5). The friend thus objectifies Wordsworth's fear and, by admitting the possibility of such an event himself, prevents it from being simply Wordsworth's own mad and solitary speculation. Like Wordsworth (and many contemporaries) he has had identical thoughts about an apocalypse. Where Wordsworth's vision had been one of earthquake and fire (29–30), the friend's story describes a 'deluge' (99). Both, in effect, swop stories of cataclysms in an age obsessed by millenarian thought. The friend's tentative comment on the likelihood of such a catastrophe (52) reflects Wordsworth's own tentativeness. It is not a constant nightmare, 'A thought is with me sometimes' (28), but there is real disquietude in the narration which follows.

The Arab of the dream carried a stone and shell; the stone was a

[101]

symbol of geometry ('Euclid's Elements' (88)), and geometry was to be an important restorative to Wordsworth's own mental health in Book X (900–4); the shell symbolising poetry ('A loud prophetic blast of harmony' (96)) was ' "something of more worth" ' (90). The Arab in his urgent quest to save both, was absorbed into the story over which the friend fell asleep, Cervantes' *Don Quixote* (59–60). Wordsworth shares the Arab's concern, while Quixote, a medieval knight-errant adrift in a modern world, frustrated by his inability to find an epic task, parallels Wordsworth's own frustration at the inability of the mind to find its proper element (44–8). The dream is vivid, concrete, detailed, and alive with implications. It has the force of a prophecy, which is what dreams were commonly held to be. The mysterious ambiguities, common to dreams, add to the complexity. The figure was 'the very knight/Whose tale Cervantes tells' but 'was an arab of the desert too' (123–5). Although the stone and shell were individually distinct, the dreamer 'Nor doubted once but that they both were books/Having a perfect faith in all that passed' (113–14).

As the 'fleet waters of the drowning world' (136) gained upon the fleeing Arab, the dreamer-friend woke up and found that he was in reality confronted by the elements of the dream, ' "I waked in terror,/And saw the sea before me, and the book/In which I had been reading at my side" ' (137–9). Whereas in the previous paragraph the Nature-culture contest had resulted in the destruction of books and in Nature victoriously re-emerging from a fiery destruction, though in a different form ('kindlings like the morning' (35)), in this paragraph the outcome of the prophetic dream is ambivalent. As the lines stand, the effect on the dreamer was either one of sheer terror as he woke to find the dream seemingly true, or of sublime peace and relief when he saw that it was only a dream after all. We never learn the outcome of the Arab's quest. Did he save the stone and shell? Or did the deluge overtake him? The feeling of unease we experience in the dream sequence is precisely because we are left guessing. The two possibilities of championing human culture successfully, or simply seeing it succumb to Nature's power, engage Wordsworth directly in the next paragraph and subsequently.

He began, therefore, with the civilised intention of writing a Book about books, but by now he has drifted into a vision of horror. He sees that Nature threatens to obliterate culture entirely. The immediate drama is to be the dilemma with which, he imagines, such a prospect might confront him personally.

Lines 140–65

The 'arab phantom' (141) haunts his imagination. Wordsworth makes some effort to identify with him as heroic book-saver. He does not feel pity so much as 'reverence' (150) for the Arab's task. If a world catastrophe happened, however, the moral dilemma would be acute. It would then be a straight choice between attempting to save either human life or culture. Wordsworth proceeds hesitantly. His love for mankind, on the one hand, pulls against his strong feelings about the irreparable destruction of civilisation on the other. Nevertheless, he seems able, for the moment, to delegate the human responsibility to others, 'Enow there are on earth to take in charge/Their wives, their children, and their virgin loves,/Or whatsoever else the heart holds dear –' (153–5). Immediately, though, comes a pause and a repetition, 'Enow to think of these' (156). The afterthought reveals a doubt. Then follows what seems a more definite statement, 'yea, will I say,/In sober contemplation of the approach/Of such great overthrow . . . I methinks/Could share that maniac's anxiousness, could go/Upon like errand' (156–61). But 'methinks' qualifies certainty. Also, '*Could* share' (our italics) is by no means definite. It only suggests what he might do. Furthermore, those numerous occasions on which he has raised the possibility to himself ('Oftentimes') have been only when he has actually *held* a volume of perhaps Shakespeare or Milton in his hand (163–5), and at no other specified time. Even then, he has been simply 'half-possessed' by 'deep entrancement' (162), not really fully awake to an actual situation. The phrase 'at least' (161) also defuses the force of 'Oftentimes'. The assertions have constant qualifications placed upon them. The innate tentativeness in the paragraph successfully conveys the uncertainty he is feeling in attempting to identify with the Arab's errand. The Arab's frantic concern is to save civilisation. Wordsworth in approaching identification with that task betrays, at the same time, a deep unease about consigning the care for humanity to others.

Lines 166–92

This paragraph sets out to bring books back into prominence after the speculations of the previous three. Nature must have been, he says, 'Mighty, indeed supreme' (166) to have kept him from cultural themes for so long. At the heart of the paragraph is the feeling that perhaps he should have given in his 'travelling back' (171) through childhood days an account of 'some tale' (178) which impressed him then and continues to affect him (179). He should have made the 'bowers' (173) of childhood 'resound' with this tale and mingled thankfulness with the 'lisping' (169) and 'prattling' (170) of childhood. Such 'thoughtless melodies' (175) of childhood, however, again divert attention from books towards the inarticulate and unliterary. The question – 'wherefore should I speak,/Why call upon a few weak words to say/What is already written in the hearts/Of all that breathe?' (184–7) puts the value of books in some doubt. Weak words are being opposed to what is 'heartfelt' (cp. 'Why should I speak of what a thousand hearts/Have felt' (IV: 33–4)), and as he had *not* included the 'simply fashioned tale' (177), the most appropriate thing he feels he can now do is to point to the 'trickling tear/Upon the cheek of listening infancy' (189–90) instead. This is the language of feeling. As so often in the poem, we are being made to consider the efficacy of words in describing emotion. He indicates his sense of an obligation to write about books, but at the same time we feel that he is not fully committed for he keeps excusing his neglect of them: 'It might have well beseemed me' (176), 'How could I ever play an ingrate's part?' (172), 'Once more should I have made those bowers resound' (173). The lines to Coleridge have an insistent, special pleading, 'O Friend! O Poet! . . . Think not that I could ever pass along/Untouched by these remembrances; no, no . . .' (180–2). The previous paragraph had concluded with books as the earthly caskets (164), the coffins, of 'immortal' verse, and with the imposing figures of Shakespeare and Milton. This one, however, has led us through simple tales and thoughtless melodies to the tears of infancy. Instead of the literary immortals ('labourers divine' (165)), Wordsworth now brings to the foreground the neglected world of the affections and the spontaneous responsiveness of children.

Lines 193–222

At the beginning of this paragraph he now does the very thing he had imagined himself as Arab book-saver preventing. He consigns books to oblivion. It seems to have been enough simply to register (194) his debt to literature. 'Whatever else . . . /Of power or pleasure' has been 'sown or fostered' (194–5), 'let that remain/Where it lies hidden in . . . the depths' (196–8). The stated theme is 'Books', but he seems to be constantly pulled towards the powerful influence he feels in Nature (222). Now, as though to set himself back on course, he begins a long sentence, 'And yet it seems/That here, in memory of all books' (198–9), concluding with, 'It seemeth (214) . . . That I should here assert their rights' (217). In the list of authors and works acknowledged there is a progressive diminution from 'Homer the great thunderer' (203), the Biblical 'voice' which 'roars' (204), and the 'trumpet-tones' that 'shake' (206) the English shores, down to the 'low and wren-like warblings' (208) of unimposing, unlettered people. There is, in other words, a gradual descent from works of epic grandeur to the more natural – to simplest tales and 'ballad tunes' (211), written not for the educated and initiated but for 'the hungry ears of little ones' (212). The paragraph descends in precisely the same way as the previous one from the one before it. And once again the descent is done in such a way as to exalt the lowly – children, 'old

men' (213), and the makers of tales, perhaps now 'sleeping nameless in their scattered graves' (216), but who are here at last given
their due 'honours' (218). He consistently states his obligation to
'assert their rights' (i.e. of books and authors) (217), 'It seemeth
(214) . . . That I should (217) . . . should once for all (218) . . .
speak of them' (219) and so on, but the paragraph descends
progressively towards 'Nature'. Finally, the 'powers' (219) of
books are to be 'hallowed – only less/ . . . Than Nature's self'
(220–2). At this point it is Nature which has stolen the climax of a
paragraph which set out to praise books.

Lines 223–45

Every argument, then, which starts out with books as the subject
seems, somehow, to veer back to Nature. In this paragraph he
embarks upon the 'transitory themes' (224) of contemporary
education which he regards as a plague, 'a pest' visited upon 'the
children of the land' (228). He opposes to this 'evil' (227) lessons
he has learnt from that imaginative literature in which natural
powers are at work, 'things that teach as Nature teaches' (231).
The emphasis falls so squarely on this that his statement, 'This
verse is dedicate to Nature's self' (230) seems a curious thing to
find in a book entitled *Books*. Both he and Coleridge had done the
same kind of reading in childhood, but the prominent images are
all derived from natural landscape, 'wandering as we did/Through
heights and hollows and bye-spots of tales' (234–5), or from
pastoral, 'happy pastures' (237), 'growing grass' (243), 'mower's
scythe' (245). This freedom to wander at will among childhood
tales, contrasts with captive contemporary children, 'followed,
watched, and noosed' (238) and allowed only to read books which
have been passed fit for consumption, just as a 'stallèd ox' (242) is
given only cut grass to eat.

In these last three paragraphs, then, Wordsworth began by first
of all considering his omissions from previous Books. 'Living
Nature' (167) has detained him from 'other thoughts' (168) and
made him, he fears, an 'ingrate' (172) to books. He wonders

whether he *should* have spoken about their influence after all (175–9). Finally he decides against any further discussion and to leave consideration of their influence endlessly hidden in Time's depths (196–8). Yet the feeling of being obliged to say something about them continues in 193–222, 'it seems', 'I should', etc. Wordsworth is showing us a mind in the process of unfolding. He feels impelled to say something that he is not entirely single-minded about.

Lines 246–90

The previous paragraph's emphasis on natural teaching is expanded here where he remembers his mother as an example of a natural teacher. She was herself, 'not falsely taught' (266) and became the 'hinge of all our learnings' (258). From the heifer and the ox we move to another animal image, 'Behold the parent hen' (246). The dignified address seems incongruous at first, but the analogy is a sound one. Like the parent hen, Wordsworth's mother showed care for her 'brood' which did not amount to an excessive concern. Her 'tenderness and love' (251) was something almost unconscious and instinctive. By way of contrast, the next paragraph will criticise the harmful effects produced by meddlesome contemporary educationalists. Wordsworth draws back from blaming them here because he does not want to introduce a note of sourness into a passage which remembers his mother. To do so would be disrespectful to her memory – 'Little suits it me/To break upon the sabbath of her rest/With any thought that looks at others' blame' (260–2). Consequently, he finds his thoughts 'checked' (264). At the same time, however, the implication is that out of respect to her teaching he should really *be* blaming them (after all, she will not hear him (266)). He finds a way out of the predicament by going on to praise her more, instead of attacking others. She derived her dignity and earth-wisdom 'from times past' (267). Her humility and selflessness belong to what seemed an older, almost Biblical, order; for example, 'Had no presumption, no such jealousy . . . was not puffed up . . . Nor selfish . . .' (269–80) echoes St Paul on charity, 'Charity suffereth long, and is kind; charity envieth not; charity vaunteth not itself, is not puffed up' (I Corinthians 13). By this point in the Book the tone has changed dramatically. The sublime voice of the prophet of doom has dwindled away and has become concerned with the domestic, the natural, and the tender; farm-yard animals (heifer, ox, hen), maternal breasts filled with 'innocent milk' (272).

Lines 290–349

At this point he recognises that the 'drift' (290) of his argument may have been unclear. He says that he has 'recoiled' (291) from depicting 'as it is' (292) the 'monster' (292) child produced by educational theorists. The word 'recoiled' looks back to 'Hence am I checked' (264) where he had refrained from attacking false teachers just as, here, he 'recoils' from attacking the products of such teachers. The 'drift' towards direct blame has not been 'obvious' because he has been hesitant to state such blame (260–2). But the remark on the uncertain direction of this drift seems to have a much wider relevance to the whole movement of the Book so far. The statement is not a naive comment of Wordsworth's in which he somehow apologises for his own confusion. What he is saying is that his direction has been uncertain because he has been in many different minds about his subject. The 'drift' is part of the consistent metaphor of his mind as 'river' (see, for example II: 214–15; IV: 39–55). A river, like the Poet's mind here, has many currents and cross-currents. We have already seen that the pattern of the previous paragraphs has been made up of convictions boldly advanced and then withdrawn. Thoughts of catastrophe have inspired determination to save books which has been immediately qualified by anxiety about leaving humanity to its fate. Open admiration for Homer, Shakespeare, or Milton has been tempered by thoughts of more humble and, in some ways, more valuable literature. The power of imaginative literature has demanded fuller treatment, only to be displaced by further speculation about

Nature. Wordsworth is presenting the mind as something truly organic.

The children he goes on to describe were the products of 'advanced' teaching methods. Rousseau, in his book *Émile* (1762),[2] had maintained that if a child were allowed to be open to natural influences and for the most part kept away from books in his early formative years, then he would grow up into an ideal adult with his mind free from prejudice. He would be a child of Nature who, because he had followed his natural instincts, would be more true and unspoiled. In the years following the publication of *Émile* there was much contemporary interest in the evolution of the ideal human being, though the emphasis tended to shift from the means employed to the end product instead. Literature was produced and techniques used to ensure that the child received the right influences. Rousseau's theories were twisted in the quest for what Wordsworth describes here as 'the monster birth/Engendered by these too industrious times' (292–3). Such a child is for him 'no child,/But a dwarf man' (294–5). The syntax is complex at this point. In 'knowledge, virtue, skill' (295) he is the 'noontide shadow of a man complete' (297), in other words, a *nonentity* ('noontide shadow') both in 'what he is not' (i.e. a child) and 'in what he is' (i.e. not a man) (296). In other words, he is neither one thing nor the other. The rhetorical complexity resolves finally into 'nothing'. This convoluted syntax is echoed in the baroque extravagance of the imagery in the rest of the paragraph, moving as it does from fountains (301), to dishes of food (305), to knights in armour (314–5), to prison-doors 'Tremendously embossed' (322), to weeds choking a pathway (324–5), to ecclesiastical prelates (325), to a throned monarch (329), all making up an indigestible confusion like the model child himself. Although he 'can read lectures upon innocence' (313) this is not an innocent activity for a child. Fear, unlike in Wordsworth's own experience, 'Touches him not' (318), and his overdeveloped 'nice . . . sense/Of the ridiculous' (307–8) produces only itself something ridiculous. In all, the sheer complexity of this paragraph is in contrast with that 'simple-mindedness' (288) on which the emphasis in the previous one falls. It is this simplicity which is echoed in the wisdom of 'old

Grandame Earth' (346), in 'playthings' (347), and the natural imagery of the concluding lines, 'in their woodland beds the flowers/Weep, and the river-sides are all forlorn' (348–9).

Lines 350–69

This child-product, then, is unnatural and unwholesome. He is like a preserved corpse (353) which keeps the appearance of freshness in its own undisturbed atmosphere, but immediately crumbles into dust in the open air. So, 'fresh and shewy' (353) though the child may be, 'Forth bring him to the air of common sense' (352) and 'the corps/Slips from us into powder' (353–4). The teacher, instead of providing enlightenment for the child, merely feeds his 'Vanity' (354) by driving him in upon himself and impounding him within the enclosure ('pinfold' (362)) of his own conceit. The word 'pound' (361), too, suggests beating, like 'Authority' in Book III, 'beating with his staff/The child that might have led him' (640–1). The restraints imposed by these busy helpers (360) are set against the imaginative open-endedness of the literature of folk and fairy-tale. Romance encourages the child to forget himself (369) in mystery. As Wordsworth will show, this can be a truly stabilising influence even if the stories themselves, 'Jack the Giant-killer', etc. (366), are rather gruesome. It is clear that Wordsworth's conception of 'common sense' (352) is a challenging one. His remedy is to foster imagination in the child by introducing him to absurd and grotesque stories. This is not what a reader might have expected by 'Forth bring him to the air of common sense' (352).

Lines 370–88

Educationalists of the kind described here are the 'mighty workmen' of 'our later age' (370), as distinct from those of a previous age, namely Sin and Death, who, in *Paradise Lost*, built a huge causeway from Hell to Earth and thus made easy man's road to damnation (see Book X: 282 ff.). Wordsworth's chosen analogy indicates the gravity of his feelings on the subject. So-called teachers of youth have 'overbridged/The froward chaos of futurity' (371–2) with a 'broad highway' (371) reminding us, too, of the 'broad way' which leads to destruction in Matthew 7: 13. The ironies are heavily underlined. These 'tutors of our youth', these 'guides', 'wardens', and 'stewards', who are 'watchful' (376–8), who 'have the art' (373), are no less than deceiving devils. For them, time is a commodity from which a profit can be made ('usury'). We think, by way of contrast, of Wordsworth's own childhood being 'wasteful' of time but still full of incident 'Whence profit may be drawn in times to come' (III: 668), that is, a different kind of profit. For him a 'wiser spirit' (385) is at work in 'the unreasoning progress of the world' (384). A comparison might be made here with the idea in Goya's etching, 'The Sleep of Reason produces Monsters' in which fantastic creatures rise from the head of the sleeping man.[3] In Wordsworth's conception it is the always watchful (376–78) or *waking* reason which produces the 'monster birth' (292). We are reminded, too, of how Wordsworth's blessed 'infant babe' (II: 237) was a natural birth fostered by the love of its mother and not by books and reason. Nature is said to be 'studious of our good' (387). In other words, unlike the 'mighty workmen' it is *truly* devoted and diligent on our behalf even in what would seem to be our wasted or 'unfruitful hours' (388). The paragraph is pointing out that there are much less wise influences at work which, like devils, are carefully contriving our downfall.

Lines 389–413

The boy of Winander, on the other hand, was a child privileged to escape the misfortunes of these model children. His experiences were private ones and he was as well-known to the 'cliffs/And islands' (389–90) as the child Wordsworth, in *his* private world, had been 'known' to 'the creeks and bays' of Cumberland (I: 594). The boy of this paragraph was also solitary, unlike the sociable model child, and his pursuits were simple and elemental. The account of him begins like a story, 'There was a boy' (389), and narrative expectations are set up as it goes along, 'And . . . And when . . . Then' (399/404/406). The only fulfilment of these expectations, however, is when we are told that the boy's awareness was unusually heightened after the owls stopped calling. There is no obvious significance in this. The experience of the boy seems to exclude our participation. What it presents is a very different kind of experience and we are required to make certain adjustments. It turns out, in fact, to be no story as such, or at best a very slim one. Instead of the long learned disquisitions of the talkative model child who 'knows' (334) and can 'read' (332) and 'spell' (333), we find sub-articulate 'peals' (401), 'halloos, and screams', 'echoes' (402), 'mirth and . . . din' (404). The knowledge of the Winander boy is different in kind. The 'voice' of the 'mountain torrents' (408–9) is like the 'murmurs' of the Derwent in Book I: 273, which became 'a voice/That flowed along my dreams' (I: 275–6). Here the 'voice' went 'far into his heart' (408). Unlike a human voice which is articulate and heard, this one is inarticulate and experienced differently by a deeper sense. The voice of the torrents which carried far into the heart of the boy has a mysterious destination, captured well by the dying cadence of line 408. It provides a contrast with the model child's precise 'Each little drop of wisdom' falling predictably 'Into the dimpling cistern of his heart' (344–5). Sound and visual imagery are insubstantial. The lake is 'glimmering' (394), and the 'quivering peals' (401) produce 'echoes' (402). The emphasis falls on what is unpredictable, as in the fishing and kite-flying of Book I (511ff.). The boy employed all his 'skill' (405) in hooting to the owls, but the skill was 'mocked' (405) when there simply 'chanced' (404) to be a pause of silence. The chance element is beyond the control of those 'Sages, who in their prescience would controul / All accidents' (380–1), and reinforced by words like 'shock', 'surprize' (407), 'unawares' (410), 'uncertain' (412). The boy's skill produced nothing conventionally 'useful' and it was only when his skill was defeated that his 'achievement' was greatest.

At the end of the paragraph the landscape sinks into the lake as the surrounding elements sink into his mind, so that the lake's and the mind's depths complement each other. A paraphrase of the last five lines would read, 'the visible scene with all its solemn imagery, received as a reflection into the lake, would enter into the boy's mind while he was unaware.' It seems that we are to see the boy as finally staring at the reflections in the steady lake. Just as, above, the 'echoes' (402) of the tumult are the 'reflections' of sound, so these are succeeded in turn by reflections or visual 'echoes'.

Lines 414–49

The Poet, then, remembers the premature death of this boy. Line 417 includes the whole cycle of his brief existence as it moves from 'The vale where he was born' to 'the churchyard' where he lies. 'There was a boy' reminds us, like 'There was a time' (*Intimations Ode*) of loss. But pondering on it long and deeply ('A full half-hour together' (412)) produces no answer, and certainly no moral inference is drawn such as we might, for example, expect to find in contemporary 'graveyard' poetry. Instead, the whole emphasis of the long sentence (416–22) is thrown on to the adverb 'Mute' at the beginning of line 422. This sublime silence rebukes any attempt to give 'meaning'. It contrasts, too, with the 'noises' of the previous paragraph, just as in Book III the silence of Newton's statue contrasted with the 'loquacity' of the clock and the 'shrill notes' of the college kitchens (49–51).

Wordsworth's thoughts, like those elsewhere 'too deep for tears', are beyond the scope of verbal expression. He can only be mute. The boy's death, we are allowed to feel, is something by which he continues to be affected deeply. He has 'oftentimes' (420) stood at the grave so rapt in thought that he can only estimate the passage of time – 'I believe . . . /A full half-hour together' (420–1). But now his thoughts turn to the remembered surroundings and to the 'village church' (424) in particular, the 'thronèd lady' (425) mentioned in Book IV: 14. Like Wordsworth she is mute, but, unlike him, 'forgetful of this boy' (426) and 'forgetful

[113]

too/Of all her silent neighbourhood of graves' (427–8). The church does not dwell on death and provides Wordsworth with a way out of the difficulty. He is, in a sense, admonished by her sublime forgetfulness. What follows are the 'gladsome sounds' (429) of life, and it is to these only that the church listens (429). Nevertheless, the memory of the boy's death does carry over into the description of the carefree playing schoolchildren who will eventually follow him to the grave. Although it is perhaps wise to concentrate on life and to forget, there is a wisdom, too, in remembering. Both 'wisdoms' are present and the boy's death is recounted in such a way as to imply that one can be forgetful without disrespect. The impressiveness of the passage lies in the very energy of its restraint – implicit in the word 'Mute' (cp. 'What need of many words?' (I: 113)).

The paragraph concludes with a prayer of hope that the focal village church may long continue to look down on children who, like Wordsworth and his contemporaries, were 'real children' (436) and victims of their passions ('bandied up and down by love and hate' (438)). Such unpretentious elemental lives shared the humility of animal life (cp. the animal images in 246ff.). Thus, Wordsworth 'herded' (433) (contrast 'Stringed . . . heifer' and 'stallèd ox' (240–2)) with 'young ones' (432) who 'might have fed upon a fatter soil/Of Arts and Letters' (434–5) but who were morally better because they did not. Since his own happy experience had proved 'pain and fear' (443) to be beneficial, Wordsworth invokes such blessings for the new generation, and in the next paragraph goes on to show how they were paradoxically stabilising forces in his own childhood. Even as he utters his hope, however, doubts intrude. Just as in Book II (33ff.) the focal stone table had become part of the smart assembly-room where an alien non-community found a shallow diversion, so the church, it is feared, may one day witness a race of 'model' schoolchildren. Real strength, on the other hand, comes from 'simplicity' (445), and whereas misguided education produces intellectual impotence, true knowledge is achieved without a 'loss of power' (449).

Lines 450–81

This paragraph describes the effect of romance literature upon a childhood experience. As he roved up and down 'Seeking I knew not what' (456) – the purposelessness is significant because the suggestion is that profound meanings often emerge from aimless pursuits – he 'chanced' (456) to cross a field from which he could see a heap of garments on the opposite shore of Lake Esthwaite. As in the Winander boy episode, a developing story creates expectations: 'Twilight was coming on' (459), 'Long I watched' (462), 'meanwhile the calm lake/Grew dark' (463–4). The 'breathless stillness' (466) makes us hold our breath in anticipation. The narrative has the ingredients of a Gothic story, but this time there *is* a climax when the dead man 'bolt upright/ Rose' (471–2). Yet even as he did so, the 'beauteous scene' (470) immediately absorbed him into itself in much the same way as the 'beauteous . . . spot' (416) absorbed the death of the Winander boy. Wordsworth's response was ideal, not morbidly emotional. The moment is Grecian rather than Gothic (a moment of beauty and not fear) because, in fact, he found that he was not horror-stricken as he might have expected to be. Notice how the particle 'even' in 'a spectre shape-/Of terror even' (472–3) distances him from the terror he only feels, in retrospect, *ought* to be appropriate in such a situation. Again the emotion is not the expected one, just as there had been no mourning or moralising in the churchyard. Tales of romance, we learn, had prepared the child for such a sight as this so that what he really saw was the naked body clothed in an 'ideal grace' (479), dignified 'like the works/Of Grecian art and purest poesy' (480–1). The result of the Gothic build-up is its completely Classical antithesis. In other words, Wordsworth suggests that the absurdities of despised irrational literature, far from upsetting him as a child, stabilised his response to the 'horror' of the drowned man and made something beautiful of it, like a Greek statue. The model child, on the other hand, kept away from romance and encouraged to be rational, would probably have had hysterics in the same situation.

Lines 482–500

He goes on to describe his early love for romance. Together with a friend he decided to 'hoard up' (494) to buy 'four large volumes' (489) of the 'Arabian Nights' tales. The hoarding up of 'joint savings' (495) until enough has been 'amassed' (495) humorously implies great treasure hoards (like something out of the Tales themselves) but probably made up of no more than a small amount of pocket money. Yet implicit in the 'league' or 'covenant' (492) (itself a romantic gesture), is an echo of the real financial enterprise of adulthood. They decided to 'lay aside/The monies we possessed' (493–4) and 'hoarded up,/And hoarded up' (498–9). Here, then, were children acting in uncharacteristic ways, hoarding up in 'spite of all temptation' (498) in order to reap the rewards of self-sacrifice. The mature reader's expectation of virtue rewarded ('Religiously did we preserve that vow' (497)) is not entirely unfounded but it is ultimately disappointed because he is told that 'firmness failed at length' (499). Childhood's typical 'failing' replaces adult 'success'. Here the failure of firmness directs us to find values elsewhere, in the simple realm of childhood, and in the ultimately unobtainable 'precious treasure' (482) and 'dear prize' (487) of romance itself. The 'little . . . slender abstract of the *Arabian Tales*' (483–4) is allowed to remain for the children a door half opening upon unrealised delight, where the 'successful' purchase of the 'four large volumes' would have somehow been unsubtle, an example of adult 'overkill'.

Lines 501–15

Wordsworth as young romantic used to return to his father's house in holiday time as though to an Ali Baba cave, 'I found/That golden store of books . . . /Open to my enjoyment once again' (502–4). The paragraph describes two activities to which he devoted his time. Fishing was a sport he pursued seriously 'armed with rod and line' (507), but he often slackened in his dedication to it and gave a 'desperate' (512) purposefulness to reading instead.

Earlier in the poem he described the process whereby 'every boyish sport' gradually became less interesting in itself and only delightful when 'collaterally attached' to the 'beauteous forms/Of Nature' (see II: 51–5). In the present Book he described how he had not, perhaps, given enough emphasis to the influence of reading on his childhood (166ff.). Here, then, he redresses the balance. Fishing and reading vied with each other for his attention. We are shown that Nature did not have quite so easy a task in getting him away from these things after all. Initially, too, sports had been synonymous with idleness. For example, the night skating in Book I continued in spite of the clock's clear and loud summons to bed. Fishing (see I: 511ff.) was one of the 'idle' activities of his playful youth, but it here imposed a duty upon him. As he poured his energy into a 'desperate' devouring of romantic stories (earlier he had put all his energy into sports), the tug of his line, presumably, gave him a 'smart reproach' (513) returning him 'an idler' (514), to the serious business of fishing. It was much more the glories of romance which attracted him, however. That 'golden store' of bright imagination 'defrauded' the day of *its* golden glory, the 'glaring sun' (510–12).

Lines 516–57

The 'dark/Invisible workmanship' of Book I (352–3) is recalled in the 'gracious spirit' (516) which comes 'invisibly . . . directing' (517–18) the writers of romance to 'works of love' (518). No obvious educational 'methods' direct them in this work and they are the very opposite of those meddling theorists in that they 'care not, know not, think not, what they do' (519). They might be the mysterious authors of the 'Arabian Nights' (520–1), or chivalric writers spinning (524) tales out of their own experiences like spiders spinning webs from their own 'bowels' (526). The emphasis falls on 'yearnings' and 'appetites' (530) which are 'Dumb' and 'hidden' (530) and which belong alike to childhood itself, 'that dubious hour,/That twilight' (536–7), and to the period of later life which precedes our resignation to a dwindling imaginative view of the world (539–46). In both periods we acknowledge as our 'friends' (547) the 'dreamers' (547) who provide our appetites with 'food' (531) (see 'devouring' (511)). Having presented at the beginning of this Book, a nightmare vision in which the forces of Nature destroy the products of the mind, Wordsworth now proclaims that the imaginative mind of the child 'hath more power than all the elements' (533). He no longer speculates – either about pre-existence ('being past' (534)) or the future (535), but is convinced of what he asserts ('But so it is' (536)) through an instinctive knowledge based on feeling (e.g. 'we feel, we feel,/We *know*' (our italics, 546–7)). Our 'simple childhood' (532), then, is elevated in its imaginative vigour to a position of sovereignty ('sits upon a throne' (532)), while the gradual loss of this power reduces most people to a state of 'meagre vassalage' (542), 'humbled down' (546) before that throne. In Book II he made the identical point that 'the first/ Poetic spirit of our human life – /By uniform controul of after years' was 'In most abated and suppressed, in some/Through every change of growth or of decay/Preeminent till death' (II: 275–80). Here, those few who retain that poetic spirit throughout are the 'Forgers of lawless tales', the lawbreakers, who refuse to be vassals and who, in sharing the 'throne' of childhood, make 'time/And seasons serve' (553–4) and the Earth 'crouch' (555) before them instead.

The confidence of this paragraph invites comparison with the fears at the beginning of the Book. There, a vision of universal destruction by two of the four elements, fire and water, is here replaced by an enduring imaginative life to which all four 'elements are potter's clay' (555). Instead of feeling dismay at the lack of a more durable element than paper for the mind to 'stamp her image on' (45), Wordsworth now asserts that tales of romance or 'something in the shape/Of these will live till man shall be no more' (528–9). They are intimations of the true sources of our greatness as they enshrine imaginative power which is revealed to us by the least likely candidates, 'dreamers . . . Imposters, drivellers, dotards' (547–9). Such figures are despised by rational philosophy but before them philosophy becomes, itself, an

irrational 'ape' (549) (cp. 'Superior beings . . . shew'd a
NEWTON as we shew an ape' (Pope, *Essay on Man* II: 31–4)).
The enduring power of Nature (the 'living presence' (33)), working through writers of romantic fiction, puts us in firm 'possession' (553) of what is fragile and gives permanence to what seemed
threatened. The imagination moulds and transforms the world it is
exercised upon like 'potter's clay'. It is the truly divine power in
man, as it is a reflection of the omnipresence of God, 'Here,
nowhere, there, and everywhere at once' (557).

Lines 558–68

Wordsworth now brings in a Platonic concept when he calls our
entry into life crossing an 'isthmus' (560) from our 'native
continent' (561) or pre-existent state (cp. Pope, 'Plac'd on this
isthmus of a middle state', *Essay on Man*, II: 3). A 'more impassioned strain' (558), he says, would trace the development in
reading habits as they reflect the maturing mind. In 501–15 he
described how in his earliest reading he would 'devour' his book,
'desperate' (512) for the story. The words, we imagine, were no
more than a medium. But as our 'cravings for the marvellous
relent' (564) we become, he says, more aware that 'words them-
selves/Move us with conscious pleasure' (567–8).

Lines 568–607

These lines go on to describe the awakening of his interest in
words as a medium. He does not centre so much upon his
response to poetry in general but upon his savouring of words and
phrases 'For *their own sakes*' (579). He is really describing the
birth of taste which was in its own way a sophisticated process.
There was an intoxication with the 'power' (579) of words. He
acquired an 'ear' (577) for the musical quality of 'words in tuneful
order' (578); also, a new sense of their intrinsic sweetness (578).
He realised the power and effectiveness of certain words and

phrases, 'phrases pleased me' (580). They could, rightly chosen, produce sentiments of 'delight' (580) or 'pomp' or 'love' (581). This effectiveness and sheer power of language to produce emotion was enjoyed by the boys as they repeated 'favorite verses' (588) in unison. Again redressing the balance, as it were (see 501–15), Wordsworth now puts emphasis upon books and not Nature. The elevated mood produced ('lifted above the ground' (591)) was the effect, not of the *landscape* here, but of the power of the words spoken aloud. They were as intoxicated as the birds were by their own bird-song (589–90). The paragraph begins with an expression of loss, but this is not so much for the *kind* of literature that moved him then – in many ways it was over-elaborate and false (593–4). It is rather for the 'raptures' (569) with which he read it. The entrancement is what he has lost; the ability to be, as it were, on 'holiday' (606) in that 'delicious world of poesy' (605), a something given in youth and making no demands upon him. Words, then, in spite of earlier judgments in favour of feeling itself (590–601). The Book has begun to reconsider the feeling itself (590–601), The Book has begun to reconsider the earlier topic of how much words are worth. The Poet cannot have been unaware of his own name's significance for his theme.

Lines 608–29

Speaking from 'heart experience' (609) he is careful to say that he writes 'in humblest sense/Of modesty' (609–10). He says that those who, like himself, 'With living Nature hath been intimate' (612) are especially singled out to receive her values present in great poetry. This gift is an 'enduring' and 'deep joy' (617) as against the more volatile kind ('ecstasy' (614)) shared with 'others' (614) and found in more 'glittering' (615) (superficial?) poetry. This paragraph provides the logical conclusion to the tension of the art/culture opposition with which the first part of the Book is concerned. Wordsworth now provides an answer to the dilemma he was burdened with by seeing art (books) not as the opposite of Nature, but as itself something which, as Shakespeare says, can share in great creating Nature since Nature makes that art (see *The Winter's Tale* IV: iv: 88ff.). The tensions which dramatised the earlier paragraphs are now resolved. Terms which were used earlier to describe Nature, are here specifically recalled and related to the function of words. In Book II, for example, he had talked of how he would stand and listen to 'sounds that . . . make their dim abode in distant winds' (327–9) and would drink the 'visionary power' (330) in his moods of 'shadowy exultation' (332). Here 'Visionary power/Attends upon the motions of the winds/Embodied in the mystery of Words;/There darkness makes abode, and all the host/Of shadowy things do work their changes there' (619–23). The pieces are exactly parallel and show us here how successful he is in bringing together the apparently diverging strands of the argument's 'drift'. Natural 'forms and substances' (625) are themselves surrounded by a 'light divine' (626), since they are seen through the medium of words. Words thus form a 'transparent veil' (626) by which Nature is surrounded, and natural objects are illuminated and glorified by words which are thought of here as a sort of light. They form 'a glory' (629) which is itself a prominent image for the transforming light of imagination.

Lines 630–7

The final paragraph descends from the rhetorical grandeur of the previous one to restore a sense of proportion. It is a prosaic conclusion, pausing both to acknowledge the importance of the theme and to hint at much that remains to be said.

Pattern of thought

Elemental forces destroy high culture in two imagined or dreamt-of cataclysms (1–48 and 49–139). This opposition of Nature and culture, in terms of final disaster, seems to be a projection of the Poet's own anxiety. He is morally and emotionally torn between a loyalty to great works of literature – Shakespeare, Milton, Homer, the Old Testament – and a loyalty to the utterly uncultivated and unlettered, the popular ballads appreciated by children and old men alike (211–13). This dilemma is presented as a divided purpose affecting the actual direction taken by the poem – the two drifts of his mind. It modulates into a consideration of what is natural, rather than artificial, in the upbringing of children (246–89), but still with hesitations and uncertainties. Suddenly (290) a turning-point is reached and the Poet plunges decisively into a condemnation of the distortions which over-cultivation can afflict on natural children. Tales of Romance are more valuable than high literature. The inarticulate and unlettered child (389–413) draws his sustenance from sub-articulate communication with the natural world. His aimless pursuits, reflecting in their way the Poet's own lack of direction at the beginning of this Book, serve a high purpose. Exposure to death (450–81), rather than confinement in a world of 'Arts and Letters' (435) strengthens imagination. From line 482 the Book is a celebration of the fairy-story world of Romance literature, fantastic stories passed on or invented by 'drivellers' and 'dotards' (549). Such is the food which the child's mind craves. Wordsworth recalls his own first awareness of words as separate entities. This was not produced by a child's reading-book, but by outdoor recitations of favourite verses in the company of a friend (568–607). What he noticed was their power to stir up emotion.

He ends by claiming that only an experience of 'living Nature' (612) will engender a true response to the 'great Nature that exists in works/Of mighty poets' (618–19). The Nature-culture opposition with which the Book began has resolved itself into a harmony. Words themselves are finally seen as a glory, or transfiguring medium, which can illuminate natural objects (625).

NOTES

Abbreviations

PW   *The Poetical Works of William Wordsworth*, ed. Ernest de
      Selincourt, 5 vols, Oxford, Clarendon Press, 1940–9.

Book I

  1 *PW* 3: 76.
  2 *PW* 2: 29.
  3 'Nothing can please many, and please long, but just representations of
general nature.' Johnson on Shakespeare, Walter Raleigh (ed.), Oxford,
1908, p.11.
  4 John Milton, *The Reason of Church Government* (1641).
  5 Edmund Burke, *A Philosophical Enquiry into the Origin of our Ideas
of the Sublime and the Beautiful* (1756).
  6 *PW* 2: 512.
  7 *PW* 5: 6.
  8 Alexander Pope, *The Rape of the Lock*, Canto III: 25–104.
  9 *PW* 5: 5.
10 *PW* 5: 3–4.
11 See John Locke, *An Essay Concerning Human Understanding* (1690),
and David Hartley, *Observations on Man* (1749).

Book II

1 E. de Selincourt (ed.), *Guide to the Lakes*, Oxford University Press, 1970, pp. 78–9.
2 *PW* 2: 220.
3 *PW* 4: 71.

Book III

1 F. L. Jones (ed.), *The Letters of Percy Bysshe Shelley*, 2 vols, Oxford, Clarendon Press, 1964, I: 577.
2 Edmund Spenser, *The Faerie Queen* III: xi: 28.

Book IV

1 *PW* 3: 34.

Book V

1 John Martin (1789–1854) – painter of such cataclysms as *The Deluge* and *The Great Day of His Wrath*, both depicting the end of the world and the destruction of civilisation. The Arab's nightmare predicament is something like that of *The Last Man*.
2 Jean-Jacques Rousseau (1712–78), French writer and philosopher.
3 Francisco Goya (1746–1828), Spanish painter.

[124]